"Addressing a hot topic in Pauline studies, Gathercole's *Defending Substitution* agrees with those who see Christ's death as one in which believers participate and as effecting apocalyptic deliverance. At the same time, he argues persuasively for the less-fashionable view that Paul also speaks of that death as substitutionary: Christ died in the place of others, and for their sins. A model of scholarly clarity and sobriety."

—**Stephen Westerholm**, McMaster University

"In this slender but admirably clear and focused volume, Simon Gathercole sets out to recover the recently unfashionable understanding of the atonement in classic Reformational terms of substitution. He concludes that there is indeed every reason to recognize this theme in key texts such as 1 Corinthians 15:3 and Romans 5:6, when they are understood in their Old Testament as well as Greco-Roman contexts. But this is for him a case of compatible rather than competing metaphors: Christ's substitution for sinners does not make his death any the less representative or liberating. I warmly recommend this revival of a classic argument that recent New Testament scholarship sometimes appears to have forgotten. Here is an eminently accessible point of reference for future exegetical, theological, and, indeed, ecumenical engagement with St. Paul on the death of Christ."

—**Markus Bockmuehl**, Keble College, Oxford

Acadia Studies in Bible and Theology

Craig A. Evans and Lee Martin McDonald, General Editors

The last two decades have witnessed dramatic developments in biblical and theological study. Full-time academics can scarcely keep up with fresh discoveries, recently published primary texts, ongoing archaeological work, new exegetical proposals, experiments in methods and hermeneutics, and innovative theological syntheses. For students and nonspecialists, these developments are confusing and daunting. What has been needed is a series of succinct studies that assess these issues and present their findings in a way that students, pastors, laity, and nonspecialists will find accessible and rewarding. Acadia Studies in Bible and Theology, sponsored by Acadia Divinity College in Wolfville, Nova Scotia, and in conjunction with the college's Hayward Lectureship, constitutes such a series.

The Hayward Lectureship has brought to Acadia many distinguished scholars of Bible and theology, such as Sir Robin Barbour, John Bright, Leander Keck, Helmut Koester, Richard Longenecker, Martin Marty, Jaroslav Pelikan, Ian Rennie, James Sanders, and Eduard Schweizer. The Acadia Studies in Bible and Theology series reflects this rich heritage.

These studies are designed to guide readers through the ever more complicated maze of critical, interpretative, and theological discussion taking place today. But these studies are not introductory in nature; nor are they mere surveys. Written by leading authorities in the field, the Acadia Studies in Bible and Theology series offers critical assessments of the major issues that the church faces in the twenty-first century. Readers will gain the requisite orientation and fresh understanding of the important issues that will enable them to take part meaningfully in discussion and debate.

Defending Substitution

An Essay on Atonement in Paul

Simon Gathercole

B **Baker Academic**
a division of Baker Publishing Group
Grand Rapids, Michigan

© 2015 by Simon Gathercole

Published by Baker Academic
a division of Baker Publishing Group
P.O. Box 6287, Grand Rapids, MI 49516-6287
www.bakeracademic.com

Printed in the United States of America

Library of Congress Cataloging-in-Publication Data
Gathercole, Simon J.
    Defending substitution : an essay on atonement in Paul / Simon Gathercole.
        pages cm. — (Acadia studies in Bible and theology)
    Includes bibliographical references and index.
    ISBN 978-0-8010-4977-4 (pbk. : alk. paper)
    1. Atonement—Biblical teaching. 2. Bible. Epistles of Paul—Criticism, interpretation, etc. 3. Bible. Corinthians, 1st, XV—Criticism, interpretation, etc. I. Title.
    BS2655.A7G27 2015
    232'.3—dc23   2014048030

Unless noted otherwise, Scripture translations are those of the author.

Scripture quotations labeled ESV are from The Holy Bible, English Standard Version® (ESV®), copyright © 2001 by Crossway, a publishing ministry of Good News Publishers. Used by permission. All rights reserved. ESV Text Edition: 2007

Scripture quotations labeled KJV are from the King James Version of the Bible.

Scripture quotations labeled NIV are from the Holy Bible, New International Version®. NIV®. Copyright © 1973, 1978, 1984, 2011 by Biblica, Inc.™ Used by permission of Zondervan. All rights reserved worldwide. www.zondervan.com

Scripture quotations labeled NRSV are from the New Revised Standard Version of the Bible, copyright © 1989, by the Division of Christian Education of the National Council of the Churches of Christ in the United States of America. Used by permission. All rights reserved.

In keeping with biblical principles of creation stewardship, Baker Publishing Group advocates the responsible use of our natural resources. As a member of the Green Press Initiative, our company uses recycled paper when possible. The text paper of this book is composed in part of post-consumer waste.

15   16   17   18   19   20   21   7   6   5   4   3   2   1

To Pete and Dirk

Contents

Preface 9

Abbreviations 11

Introduction 13

The Importance of Substitution

Defining Substitution: Christ in Our Place

Criticisms of Substitution

1. Exegetical Challenges to Substitution 29

The Tübingen Understanding of Representative
"Place-Taking"

Interchange in Christ

Apocalyptic Deliverance

The Omission or Downplaying of "Sins"

Conclusion

**2. "Christ Died for Our Sins according to the Scriptures"
(1 Cor. 15:3) 55**

The Importance of 1 Corinthians 15:3–4

"According to the Scriptures"

Substitution in 1 Corinthians 15:3
Conclusion

**Excursus: An Objection—Why, Then, Do Christians
Still Die?   80**

3. **The Vicarious Death of Christ and Classical Parallels
   (Rom. 5:6–8)   85**

   The Translation of Romans 5:6–8
   A Sketch of the Exegesis
   Vicarious Deaths in Classical Tradition
   The Comparison in Romans 5:6–8
   Conclusion

Conclusion   109
Bibliography   115
Index of Subjects   122
Index of Authors   124
Index of Scripture and Other Ancient Sources   126

Preface

This book originated in a request from Francis Watson (my colleague at the time in Aberdeen) to present a paper in the Pauline Soteriology section at the Society of Biblical Literature Annual Meeting in Washington, DC, in 2006. I am grateful to Francis for this and also to John Webster (now at the University of St. Andrews) and Miroslav Volf (Yale University) for responding to the paper. This paper then underwent a process of binary fission in which the material on 1 Corinthians 15 and Romans 5 became separated into two lectures. I am thankful to the faculty of Concordia Theological Seminary (especially Charles Gieschen) in Fort Wayne, Indiana, for the invitation to deliver the lectures at their Annual Symposium on Exegetical Theology and Annual Symposium on the Lutheran Confessions in January 2008. In 2010 the material expanded into three lectures, which were given as the Annual Biblical Studies Lectures at Campbellsville University, Kentucky, at the kind invitation of Jarvis Williams. Some of the material was also presented at Tyndale University, Toronto, 2011, and as the Robert Saucy Lectures at Biola University, thanks to Ben Reynolds and Clinton Arnold, respectively. Last and by no means least, I am grateful to Craig Evans for the opportunity to give the material here as the Hayward Lectures at Acadia University in 2011, and to publish them in the Acadia Studies in Bible and Theology series.

I am also grateful to those who have read parts of this book in its written form. Morna Hooker, Dan Bailey, and Richard Bell kindly read parts of chapter 1 and helped me avoid various misunderstandings. David Shaw read the introduction and chapter 1, and James Carleton Paget went well beyond the call of duty in reading the whole manuscript.

In writing the book I was concerned not to sacrifice too much the accessibility that was necessary to a series of public lectures, and so I have tried to stick as closely as possible to their original style in order to make the argument as easily comprehensible as possible, both in clarity and brevity. The argument here is of course only a rather cursory one, and I readily anticipate reviewers' criticisms that I have omitted this or that passage that might have supported or damaged my case, or omitted responding to this or that objection that could be lodged against the argument. Others might complain that I have not set the Pauline evidence in its larger theological framework or the individual passages in their wider literary context. I can only respond that if one were to do all of that, the book would have had to multiply enormously in size. On Callimachus's principle that "a big book is a big evil" (μέγα βιβλίον μέγα κακόν), I hope that the brevity of this book is more an advantage than a disadvantage.

I would like to dedicate this book to fellow musketeers Dirk Jongkind and Pete Williams. It has been a privilege (as well as great fun) speaking together with them at *Bible and Church* events over the past few years. Long may our friendship continue.

Abbreviations

A.H.	Irenaeus, *Against Heresies*
AJA	*American Journal of Archaeology*
Alc.	Euripides, *Alcestis*
CBQ	*Catholic Biblical Quarterly*
Diss.	Epictetus, *Dissertationes*
Fab.	Hyginus, *Fabulae*
IG	*Inscriptiones graecae*
IGBulg	*Inscriptiones graecae in Bulgaria repertae*
IJST	*International Journal of Systematic Theology*
Il.	Homer, *Iliad*
JHS	*Journal of Hellenic Studies*
JSNT	*Journal for the Study of the New Testament*
JTS	*Journal of Theological Studies*
KEK	Kritisch-exegetischer Kommentar über das Neue Testament
LCL	Loeb Classical Library
Mor.	Plutarch, *Moralia*
NIGTC	New International Greek Testament Commentary
NovT	*Novum Testamentum*
NTS	*New Testament Studies*

OCD[3]	*Oxford Classical Dictionary*. Edited by S. Hornblower and A. Spawforth. 3rd ed. Oxford: Oxford University Press, 1996
Off.	Cicero, *De officiis*
P. Hercul.	Papyrus Herculanensis
PIBA	Proceedings of the Irish Biblical Association
Pr. Man.	Prayer of Manasseh
Pyth.	Iamblichus, *Life of Pythagoras*
SBET	*Scottish Bulletin of Evangelical Theology*
SJT	*Scottish Journal of Theology*
Spec. Leg.	Philo, *De specialibus legibus*
Tusc. Disp.	Cicero, *Tusculanae disputationes*
TynBul	*Tyndale Bulletin*
V.P.	Diogenes Laertius, *Vitae philosophorum*
WUNT	Wissenschaftliche Untersuchungen zum Neuen Testament
ZNW	*Zeitschrift für die neutestamentliche Wissenschaft und die Kunde der älteren Kirche*
ZTK	*Zeitschrift für Theologie und Kirche*

Introduction

Were you there when they crucified my Lord?" goes the opening line of the old spiritual. I sometimes remark to students that, out of its original context, there are two possible answers to this question. The question—ambiguous as it is—probably is a *nonne* question, expecting the answer "yes." In that sense, the answer might presuppose Christian identification with Christ on the cross or participation in his death, a human participation grounded in the fact that in his death Christ *represents* us. "We have *died with* Christ" (Rom. 6:8).

On the other hand, one might also answer "no" to the question. It was an event that took place before the church's very existence. Christ died *alone*, as illustrated by the fact that, on his arrest, he insisted that the disciples were not to accompany him (John 18:8–9). In a crucial sense, then, we were *not* there. He *was* there, taking our place in our stead.

The former understanding of Christ's death—as a representative act in which believers participate—has become an uncontroversial axiom in biblical scholarship and Christian theology. The latter, on the other hand, has become highly contested. It is in the light of this controverted status of "substitution" that this book

13

aims to argue that Christ's death for our sins *in our place*, *instead of us*, is in fact a vital ingredient in the biblical (in the present discussion, Pauline) understanding of the atonement. It should be emphasized, however, that the argument here does nothing to undermine the importance of representation and participation. Rather, the point is that substitution can happily coexist with them.

1. The Importance of Substitution

Why such a focus on substitution? In my view, substitutionary atonement is an important doctrine for at least two reasons.[1] First, it is vital to our understanding of what the New Testament says about the death of Christ and the gospel, and such understanding is a clear necessity for the church and for biblical scholarship. For Christians today, being clear on what it means that Christ died for our sins is essential both to the Christian's relationship with God as well as for the communication of the gospel. Second, substitution has often also been held to have important pastoral implications.[2] To take just one example, it is frequently thought to be vital to Christian assurance. As Calvin argued,

> We must specially remember this substitution in order that we may not be all our lives in trepidation and anxiety, as if the just vengeance, which the Son of God transferred to himself, were still impending over us.[3]

If this is right, it illustrates the pastoral importance of substitution: knowing that Christ has died in our place means that we

1. See further the theological implications of substitution drawn in G. Röhser, *Stellvertretung im Neuen Testament* (Stuttgart: Verlag Katholisches Bibelwerk, 2002), 128–45.

2. This is not at the expense of other dimensions of the atonement. Some pastoral implications of participation, for example, are drawn out in passages such as Romans 6 and Hebrews 4.

3. Calvin, *Institutes* 2.16.5, quoted in M. Davie, "Dead to Sin and Alive to God," *SBET* 19 (2001): 162.

need no longer fear that we are still in our sins. The first matter that must be dealt with in any discussion like this, however, is to define the key term. What exactly is substitution?

2. Defining Substitution: Christ in Our Place

I am defining *substitutionary* atonement for the present purposes as Christ's death in our place, instead of us. The "instead of us" clarifies the point that "in our place" does not, in substitution at least, mean "in our place *with us*." (Jesus was, for example, baptized *in our place with us*—that is, the baptism was not a substitution.) In a substitutionary theory of the death of Jesus, he did something, underwent something, so that we did not and would never have to do so. This definition can be generally agreed upon; although there is considerable debate about the validity of substitution as an aspect of the atonement in Scripture (as well as a good deal of caricature of the idea), there is not so much debate about what substitution is.

We can illustrate this definition with some individual comments, here from Martin Luther, Robert Letham, and Karl Barth. We begin with Luther, who argues the following:

> Paul guarded his words carefully and spoke precisely. And here again a distinction must be made; Paul's words clearly show this. For he does not say that Christ became a curse on his own account, but that he became a curse "for us." Thus the whole emphasis is on the phrase "for us." For Christ is innocent in so far as his own person is concerned; therefore he should not have been hanged from the tree. But because, according to the Law, every thief should have been hanged, therefore, according to the Law of Moses, Christ himself should have been hanged, for he bore the person of a sinner and a thief—and not of one but of all sinners and thieves. For we are sinners and thieves, and therefore we are worthy of death and eternal damnation. But Christ took all our sins upon himself, and for them he died on the cross. Therefore it was appropriate for

him to become a thief and, as Isaiah says (53:12), to be "numbered with the thieves." . . . He has and bears all the sins of all men in his body—not in the sense that he has committed them but in the sense that he took these sins, committed by us, upon his own body, in order to make satisfaction for them with his own blood.[4]

When the merciful Father saw that we were being oppressed through the Law, that we were being held under a curse, and that we could not be liberated from it by anything, he sent his Son into the world, heaped all the sins of all men upon him, and said to him: "Be Peter, the denier; Paul, the persecutor, blasphemer and assaulter; David, the adulterer; the sinner who ate the apple in Paradise; the thief on the cross. In short, be the person of all men, the one who has committed the sins of all men. And see to it that you pay and make satisfaction for them." Now the Law comes and says: "I find him a sinner, who takes upon himself the sins of all men. I do not see any other sins than those in him. Therefore let him die on the Cross."[5]

If the sins of the entire world are on that one man, Jesus Christ, then they are not on the world. But if they are not on him, then they are still on the world. Again, if Christ himself is made guilty of all the sins that we have all committed, then we are absolved from all sins. . . . But if he is innocent and does not carry our sins, then we carry them and shall die and be damned in them.[6]

In his commentary on Galatians 3:13 here, Luther uses a series of graphic images in the course of his affirmation of substitution and his polemic against the view that Christ's death is a mere moral example. Luther's stance is clear. In the first paragraph above, Christ took the place of us sinners and thereby took our sins upon himself so that they no longer rested upon us. In the eyes of the law, Christ's bearing of our sins means that sin is not reckoned to

4. J. Pelikan, ed., *Luther's Works*, vol. 26, *Lectures on Galatians (1535)* (St. Louis: Concordia, 1968), 277.

5. Ibid., 280.

6. Ibid.

our account. And in the final statement, similarly, Christ's bearing of our sins means that we do not bear them.

We can also consider the rather more prosaic statements of Letham and Barth:

> Christ himself willingly submitted to the just penalty which we deserved, receiving it on our behalf and in our place so that we will not have to bear it ourselves.[7]

> In his doing this for us, in his taking to himself—to fulfil all right-eousness—our accusation and condemnation and punishment, in his suffering in our place and for us, there came to pass our reconciliation with God.[8]

These definitions contain several of the key phrases associated with substitution. Luther drew the contrast between Christ not becoming a curse on his own account but for us; he takes our sins on his own body. In the definition from Letham, "on our behalf and in our place" is certainly expressing the point, with the further clarification "so that we will not have to bear it ourselves." The phrase "in our place and for us" in Barth's statement conveys the same idea because of Jesus's removal of the accusation from us onto himself.

In other words, what will be argued in this book is that when Christ died bearing our sins or guilt or punishment, he did so *in our place* and *instead of us*. In a vital sense—as Luther put it—when Christ was bearing our sins, that meant that we were not bearing our sins and do not have to do so. Speaking more grammatically, substitution is often expressed in the alternation between the third-person singular "he" (Christ) and the first-person plural "us." As in Letham's definition above, "*Christ himself* willingly submitted to the just penalty which *we* deserved." And in Barth: "In *his* doing

---

7. R. Letham, *The Work of Christ* (Leicester: Inter-Varsity, 1993), 133.
8. K. Barth, *Church Dogmatics* IV/1, *The Doctrine of Reconciliation* (Edinburgh: T&T Clark, 1956), 223.

this *for us*, in *his taking to himself*—to fulfil all righteousness—*our* accusation and condemnation and punishment, in *his* suffering in *our* place and for *us*." He did something, underwent something, so *we* did not—and never will—have to.

Although these definitions typically understand substitution in terms of substitutionary punishment, the matter of what precisely it was that Christ bore in our stead will not be treated here in the present study.[9] As Finlan has insightfully delineated, there are various types of substitution in the Bible.[10] For the purposes of brevity and clarity, it is also left open here what Christ's substitutionary death in our place entails. A number of elements of the atonement—propitiation, punishment of sin, representation, expiation, for example—that are often taken together may indeed rightly be taken together, but it is important to recognize that *each* of them must be derived from Scripture and not be seen merely as mutually entailing. Substitution is logically distinguishable from related concepts such as penalty, representation, expiation, and propitiation. This is not to say that they cannot all belong together in a full-orbed understanding of the atonement. But it is to say that each must arise out of exegesis and can, indeed should, be the subject of investigation in its own right. They are logically distinct rather than a priori inseparable.

2.1. Substitution and Penalty

First, one can have substitution without that being *penal* substitution, that is, without *punishment* for sins involved.[11] These

9. I have discussed it elsewhere, in my "Justified by Faith, Justified by His Blood: The Evidence of Romans 3:21–4:25," in *Justification and Variegated Nomism*, vol. 2, *The Paradoxes of Paul*, ed. D. A. Carson, P. T. O'Brien, and M. A. Seifrid (Tübingen: Mohr Siebeck; Grand Rapids: Baker Academic, 2004), 147–84.

10. See S. Finlan, *The Background and Content of Paul's Cultic Atonement Metaphors* (Atlanta: Society of Biblical Literature, 2004), e.g., 178: "*substitution* can be cultic, judicial, or economic, that is, it can be abstract, penal, or monetary." Cf. also the different forms of substitution discussed in Röhser, *Stellvertretung im Neuen Testament*, 48–57.

11. As in the conclusions of, e.g., D. W. Snyder Belousek, *Atonement, Justice, and Peace: The Message of the Cross and the Mission of the Church* (Grand Rapids:

are often treated together: what is taken *in our stead* is the penalty for sins. Substitution is not always necessarily that, however. In the case of the Old Testament scapegoat, for instance, one has a clear enough example of substitutionary expiation, that is, where the goat is a substitute for the people, bearing their sins and thereby eliminating those sins. The scapegoat, however, is not clearly bearing the penalty; it is not explicitly a penal substitution. As Leviticus 16 puts it,

> Then Aaron shall lay both his hands on the head of the live goat, and confess over it all the iniquities of the people of Israel, and all their transgressions, all their sins, putting them on the head of the goat, and sending it away into the wilderness by means of someone designated for the task. (Lev. 16:21)

The sins, therefore, are put on the head of the goat, but these sins are then carried away rather than punished in the goat. Similarly, Christ's death could in theory be described as a nonpenal substitution: in parallel to Shakespeare's Olivia leading her graces to the grave (and depriving the world of them),[12] Christ might simply have borne *our sins* away to the grave (thus saving the world from them). Whether substitutionary atonement should be described *specifically* in terms of *penal* substitution needs to be argued exegetically rather than being seen merely as a logical corollary of substitution *per se*. In a quite different way again, one Reformed theologian, John McLeod Campbell, offered an account of the atonement centered on Christ's substitutionary *penitence* rather than his bearing the guilt incurred by our sins.[13] It is less evident how this would relate to Christ's death on the cross, however.

Second, conversely, one can have punishment or penalty without substitution. We will see an example later of a view according

---

Eerdmans, 2012), 93. I am grateful to Daniel P. Bailey for drawing my attention to this book.

12. *Twelfth Night* I.5.530.

13. See discussion in O. Crisp, "Non-Penal Substitution," *IJST* 9 (2007): 415–33.

to which Jesus identifies with us in our condemnation (chap. 1, §1). In this view of the atonement we have Christ sharing in the judgment of God, but this is not in our place in the sense that he bears it and we do not. Rather, on this view, he would bear it *with us* (rather than *instead of us*) and accomplish atonement that way. Because he identifies with us so completely—not just in the incarnation but also in sharing the penalty of sin in death—he thereby represents us to God. Representation itself is not the same as substitution, however.

2.2. Substitution and Representation

Substitution entails the concept of replacement, X taking the place of Y and thereby ousting Y: the place that Y previously occupied is now filled by X. In representation, X in one sense occupies the position of Y, as in substitution. There are differences, however. In representation, X does not thereby oust Y but rather embodies Y. Indeed, it is usually a presupposition of representation that X belongs to group Y, and so the representative is *part* of the body represented. (One can also have plural representatives of a single body, as in the delegation to Gaius of which Philo of Alexandria was a part.) When a British Member of Parliament speaks and votes in the House of Commons, she speaks and votes—in theory at least—representing the members of her constituency, *of which she is one herself*. She is representing a group to which she herself belongs.[14]

14. In a sense one might argue that representation necessarily involves an element of substitution. At least in the example of British MPs, only one out of around 100,000 people in total (around 60,000 voters) is actually present in the parliamentary chamber. The same applies, *mutatis mutandis*, with members of the US House of Representatives and of the parliament in the Canadian House of Commons. In the UK, that single Member of Parliament is—in one sense—substituting for the 99,999 people who are not present.

It is possible that one can find an even more substitutionary sort of representation. As we will see below, some scholars argue that when Old Testament priests lay one hand on the bull for the sin offering, the death of the bull thereby represents the death of a priest (Lev. 4:4). If this is the case (I leave this open), then this is an

2.3. Substitution and Propitiation

Propitiation is often regarded as an important theme in Christian theology and regularly seen as closely related to, and even inseparable from, substitution. "Propitiation" within a Christian context means averting, or turning aside, the wrath of God, such that God makes himself "propitious" again. But it equally means, outside of a Christian framework, the appeasement of a pagan god. While it may turn out to be the case that the biblical picture brings substitution and propitiation into relationship with one another, there is no logical necessity *intrinsic* to these concepts that requires them to come together. This can be illustrated from the standard classical example of propitiation. Agamemnon, probably a mythical person, was king of Mycenae and commander in chief of the Greek expedition in the Trojan War. However, he had to sacrifice his daughter Iphigenia to enable the Greeks to embark on the Trojan War.[15] Prior to this, Agamemnon had somehow offended the goddess Artemis—according to one version, he had killed a stag in her sacred grove and boasted about it, and so incurred her anger.[16] Therefore, to avert the wrath of Artemis, Agamemnon had to offer the sacrifice of his daughter. This daughter, Iphigenia, was not a sacrifice in place of something else except in the very indirect sense that she was a sacrifice *in the place of* Agamemnon's hubristic offense against Artemis. Propitiations could also be quite different things altogether, as in the following case where an inscription is erected to appease a Persian fertility goddess:

> Glykia, daughter of Agrios, has been punished by Anaitis from Metro (with a disease) in her buttock; subsequently she sought out the goddess and asked her (what to do), and she erected this stone.[17]

---

indirect form of representation that is difficult—though not impossible—to separate from substitution. If it is in symbolic terms a representation, it is in another sense a substitution: the bull dies, whereas the priest does not.

15. See the helpful summary of different versions of the story in C. Sourvinou-Inwood, "Iphigenia," *OCD*[3], 765–66.

16. Sophocles, *Electra* 566–69; cf. Aeschylus, *Agamemnon* 134–38.

17. A. Chaniotis, "Illness and Cures in the Greek Propitiatory Inscriptions and Dedications of Lydia and Phrygia," in *Ancient Medicine in Its Socio-Cultural Context:*

In this case, the inscription itself appears to be the propitiation. Here again, then, propitiation is logically distinct from substitution.

Conversely, it is also the case that substitution does not necessarily entail propitiation. This can again be illustrated by the biblical "scapegoat," which is clearly a substitute but not self-evidently a propitiatory one. The scapegoat eliminates the contamination of sin but is not—at least not directly—a propitiation. It is at least unclear that the scapegoat is a propitiatory offering to YHWH.[18] Indeed, substitution is such a common concept in virtually every culture that it has a great number of applications: outside the sphere of propitiation, it even appears in football matches.

2.4. Substitution and Satisfaction

One could add *satisfaction* as another concept separable from substitution, though substitutionary theories of the atonement are sometimes confused with the satisfaction theory of Anselm.[19] They are distinct, however, because one could in theory offer satisfaction oneself for sins. This could be through serving punishment, as in the common idea that having "done one's time," one has paid for the crime; in the biblical sphere, Israel's exile comes to an end when "her hard service has been completed," on the grounds "that her sin has been paid for, that she has received from the LORD's hand double for all her sins" (Isa. 40:2). Similarly, through Israel's exile, the land experiences the requisite Sabbath rests that Israel had not allowed it (Lev. 26:34–35). Alternatively, satisfaction could be possible through—as in Kant's view to be mentioned below—the offer of compensatory obedience of one's own.

Papers Read at the Congress Held at Leiden University 13–15 April 1992, ed. H. F. J. Horstmanshoff, P. J. van der Eijk, and P. H. Schrijvers (Amsterdam: Rodopi, 1995), 2:329.

18. It is possible that the scapegoat is conceived in Leviticus as a propitiatory offering "to Azazel," though this is by no means certain.

19. I first encountered this in an article by Giles Fraser in the *Guardian*: "The technical theological term for this nasty perversion of the Easter story is penal substitution. It was dreamt up by Anselm in the 11th century and later added to by Calvin" ("Cross Purposes," April 4, 2007, http://www.theguardian.com/commentisfree/2007/apr/04/christrecrucified).

There are further distinctions that could be drawn, but these are sufficient for the present. The point here, then, is merely to focus on substitution in the sense that Christ died instead of us, in our place. The investigation here is to be focused not on these other themes but quite narrowly and specifically on substitution. We will go on to see that atonement in the Bible—at least, specifically in Paul—is to be understood not only in terms of Christ's taking our place as a *representative* but also in Christ's taking our place as a *substitute*. To repeat the point noted earlier, the aim here is not to say that Scripture teaches substitution rather than representation but to say that both are important parts of biblical teaching.

3. Criticisms of Substitution

As is well known, however, this doctrine of substitutionary atonement has come under attack by theologians on a number of different fronts over many decades, even centuries, now. The present summary is by no means intended as a proper response to all such criticisms but serves to clarify the task of the present book and also to note some of the presuppositions that either surface in biblical exegesis or that lie below the surface but may exert some influence upon it.

3.1. Theological Criticisms

We can begin with several criticisms of substitution made by those operating with Christian categories in their own discussions of the doctrine of salvation.

A Legal Fiction?

Theologians have sometimes attacked substitution as a legal fiction. How can justice really be said to be done if the guilty person is let off and an innocent bystander condemned instead?[20]

20. For a recent statement of the objection, see D. A. Campbell, *The Deliverance of God* (Grand Rapids: Eerdmans, 2009), 25.

Indeed, does not Exodus itself say, "Keep far from a false charge, and do not kill the innocent and those in the right, for I will not acquit the guilty" (Exod. 23:7)? Some have responded at this point that the "legal fiction" objection presupposes a highly individualistic and atomistic understanding of human identity, a view of identity that other parts of Scripture might challenge or at least qualify.[21]

An Immoral Doctrine?

Or again, substitutionary atonement has been accused of being not only a legal fiction but also immoral. (This is usually targeting a specifically *penal* substitutionary understanding of the cross.) In 1991, the Australian churchman Peter Carnley wrote that the idea of Christ dying in our place is not part of orthodox Christian faith. This view of the cross leads to a picture of God "of a morally repugnant kind, whose Son becomes the hapless victim of his Father's righteous anger."[22] Or in Britain, Steve Chalke emphasizes the point that the death of Christ has nothing to do with a form of "cosmic child abuse" where God "suddenly decides to vent his anger and wrath on his own Son."[23] Often such criticisms—like this one—are extremely shallow, however; they amount to little more than people saying, "I don't like this doctrine."

Three brief points can help to address the charge that Jesus is the "hapless victim" of "cosmic child abuse." First, such theological criticisms neglect the obvious fact that the death of Christ is not that of a third party but is the "self-substitution of God."[24] Outside of a context of high Christology or of the doctrine of

21. See, e.g., S. Holmes, "Can Punishment Bring Peace? Penal Substitution Revisited," *SJT* 58 (2005): 120–22, and cf. Röhser's response to Kant, noted below.

22. P. Carnley, *Anglican Messenger*, July and November 1991, cited in M. Ovey, "The Cross, Creation and the Human Predicament," in *Where Wrath and Mercy Meet: Preaching the Atonement Today*, ed. D. Peterson (Carlisle: Paternoster, 2002), 103n9.

23. S. Chalke and A. Mann, *The Lost Message of Jesus* (Grand Rapids: Zondervan, 2006), 182.

24. The title of chap. 6 of J. R. W. Stott, *The Cross of Christ* (Leicester: Inter-Varsity, 2006).

the Trinity, substitution might of course be open to such charges as those leveled above. But as far as I can see, most theologians seriously advocating substitution also hold to a high Christology.[25] Second, and related to this first point, Jesus offers himself as a sacrifice *in line with his own will*. To give two examples from Galatians, the Son "gave himself for our sins" and "loved me and gave himself for me," as Paul puts it (Gal. 1:4; 2:20). He is not simply passive victim but active agent. Third, a response can also be offered that is more subjective but still significant (and certainly no more subjective than the assertions of Carnley and Chalke). Simeon Zahl has rightly noted that it is all very well caricaturing certain atonement theories as cruel, violent, unjust, and the like, but this is not how millions of Christians over the centuries have experienced such teaching. "The vehemence of reactions against substitutionary and forensic models over the centuries has often obscured recognition of their sheer effectiveness in a wide variety of contexts and over many centuries."[26] Or as John Lennox has put it, in response to similar assertions by Dawkins and others, "In spite of the hopelessness of their position, many prominent atheists content themselves with crude, dismissive, and puerile caricatures of the very message that, for centuries, has brought hope, forgiveness, peace of mind and heart, and power for living to multitudes of ordinary men and women."[27]

25. See, e.g., Röhser, *Stellvertretung im Neuen Testament*, 43, on the relationship between Christ and God in substitutionary atonement.

26. S. Zahl, "Atonement," in *The Oxford Handbook of Theology and Modern European Thought*, ed. N. Adams, G. Pattison, and G. Ward (Oxford: Oxford University Press, 2013), 637. He further points out "the substantial divide between much academic theology and the beliefs and practices of the world's lay Christians. It is remarkable that a huge number of the world's Christians, particularly in Protestant and charismatic traditions, continue to recognize themselves far more in the experiences of Francke and Wesley from the late 17th and early 18th centuries than in the accounts provided by mainstream academic theology, where there has long been widespread discomfort with retributive and forensic models" (652).

27. J. Lennox, *Gunning for God: Why the New Atheists Are Missing the Target* (Oxford: Lion, 2011), 145.

3.2. Philosophical Objections

Much of the present questioning of substitutionary atonement has its origins in the philosophy of Immanuel Kant, especially his *Religion within the Boundaries of Mere Reason* (first edition, 1793).[28] Kant rejects a view of atonement based on substitution in favor of an exemplary understanding.[29] He expresses his difficulty with a substitutionary account as follows:

> Moreover, so far as we can judge by our reason's standards of right, this original debt, or at any rate the debt that precedes whatever good a human being may ever do . . . cannot be erased by somebody else. For it is not a *transmissible* liability which can be made over to somebody else, in the manner of a financial debt (where it is all the same to the creditor whether the debtor himself pays up, or somebody else for him), but the *most personal* of all liabilities, namely a debt of sins which only the culprit, not the innocent, can bear, however magnanimous the innocent might be in wanting to take the debt upon himself for the other.[30]

Although Kant's view has some dimensions of complexity here,[31] his principal assertion is clear: the guilt of sinning is too inseparably my own for another to take it upon himself.

28. Known variously in English as *Religion within the Limits/Bounds/Boundaries of Reason Alone/Pure Reason/Mere Reason*. The German title is *Die Religion innerhalb der Grenzen der blossen Vernunft*.

29. P. Rossi, "Kant's Philosophy of Religion," *Stanford Encyclopedia of Philosophy*, http://plato.stanford.edu/entries/kant-religion/.

30. I. Kant, *Religion within the Boundaries of Mere Reason*, in *Religion and Rational Theology*, ed. A. Wood and G. Di Giovanni, Cambridge Edition of the Works of Immanuel Kant (Cambridge: Cambridge University Press, 1996), 113. For discussion, see P. L. Quinn, "Christian Atonement and Kantian Justification," *Faith and Philosophy* 3 (1986): 440–62; G. Wenz, *Geschichte der Versöhnungslehre in der evangelischen Theologie der Neuzeit*, Münchener Monographien zur historischen und systematischen Theologie (Munich: Kaiser, 1984), 1:223–35; Röhser, *Stellvertretung im Neuen Testament*, 11–16; and B. Janowski, "He Bore Our Sins: Isaiah 53 and the Drama of Taking Another's Place," in *The Suffering Servant: Isaiah 53 in Jewish and Christian Sources*, ed. B. Janowski and P. Stuhlmacher, trans. D. P. Bailey (Grand Rapids: Eerdmans, 2004), 50–52.

31. In two ways: (a) he uses the vicarious atonement of Christ as a picture of how the transformed moral person in a sense makes compensation for the previous sins of the same person in his untransformed state, and (b) Kant does not completely

Kant's central claim here has been repeated in more recent times in Christopher Hitchens's famous attacks on Christianity. As Hitchens puts it, "Many of the teachings of Christianity are, as well as being incredible and mythical, immoral. I would principally wish to cite the concept of vicarious redemption, whereby one's own responsibilities can be flung onto a scapegoat and thereby taken away."[32] The fundamental problem with "scapegoating," he says, is that "I cannot absolve you of your responsibilities. It would be immoral of me to offer, and immoral of you to accept."[33] The charge of "immorality" here is not an accusation of cruelty, as in the objections of Carnley and Chalke noted above. Rather, Hitchens lambasts an abdication of moral responsibility on the part of the sinner and a complicity in this on the part of the would-be substitute.

Some of these criticisms will resurface in the exegetical criticisms of substitution, especially in the German sphere. As an insider to this German discussion of the atonement has noted, however, we should pause "before we accept uncritically this subject-centered theory of guilt, which makes the sinner merciless toward himself and blind to the 'other' who might be more accommodating toward him."[34] As Janowski implies here, Kant's view threatens both the freedom and the mercy of God if Christ is simply not permitted to be a substitute.[35]

3.3. A Logical Objection

One further potential obstacle to the coherence of a substitutionary atonement lies in the following objection: If Christ died

---

rule out the imputation of an alien righteousness (equivalent, for Kant, to dealing with the debt of sins) but nevertheless regards this as "completely inexplicable to human reason" (Quinn, "Christian Atonement and Kantian Justification," 452, 454).

32. C. Hitchens and D. Wilson, *Is Christianity Good for the World? A Debate* (Moscow, ID: Canon, 2008), 22.

33. C. Hitchens, *God Is Not Great: How Religion Poisons Everything* (London: Atlantic, 2008), 211.

34. Janowski, "He Bore Our Sins," 51.

35. Röhser, *Stellvertretung im Neuen Testament*, 17, also objects to the individualistic notion of personhood inherent in the Kantian framework.

in the place of believers, why do they still die? The answer to this is an exegetical one, and so it will be dealt with in an excursus between chapters 2 and 3, which discuss Paul's letters.

3.4. Exegetical Challenges

A response that one might make to any such challenges is that biblical exegesis simply demands substitution; therefore it cannot be avoided.[36] This leads directly to the most important criticisms of substitutionary atonement, namely, the repeated statements that it is actually unbiblical. These charges are the focus of the present book. The subsequent chapters will attempt to show that even the most weighty exegetical criticisms leveled at substitution are unfounded and that there is actually very good evidence for seeing substitutionary atonement as intrinsic to the biblical presentation of how God has reconciled the world to himself in Christ. The book will not range very widely across the biblical material but will rather be quite narrowly focused on Paul, which is where most of the controversy takes place. Even then, following the lectures on which this book is based, the exegesis will be confined to two case studies in chapters 2 and 3, where 1 Corinthians 15 and Romans 5 will be tackled in detail. Before that exegesis, however, we will examine some of the construals of Paul's understanding of the atonement that provide alternatives to substitution.

36. Holmes, "Can Punishment Bring Peace?," 122.

1

Exegetical Challenges to Substitution

As has already been suggested in the introduction, there is a strong tendency in current scholarship on Paul to resist seeing Christ's death as in our place, instead of us. Rather, scholars prefer a view of Christ's death *with* us—where he identifies with us rather than dying a unique death alone for us. Indeed, the point that Christ's death is representative and therefore not substitutionary can often just be made briefly in passing, as if it were understood to be an uncontroversial thought. Robert Jewett's commentary on Romans is perhaps typical in this respect: he regards it simply as having been demonstrated that the cross in Paul is to be understood in representative rather than substitutionary categories.[1]

1. R. Jewett, *Romans: A Commentary*, Hermeneia (Minneapolis: Fortress, 2006), 362: "As Daniel Powers has shown, however, the widely used formula of Christ dying in behalf of others should be understood 'in terms of representation and not in terms of substitution,'" citing D. G. Powers, *Salvation through Participation: An Examination of the Notion of the Believers' Corporate Unity with Christ in Early Christian Soteriology* (Leuven: Peeters, 2001), 233.

Rather than deal with individual statements across the board in Pauline scholarship, however, I propose to examine in more detail some of the more extensive cases made against substitution. (Again, the aim is by no means to supplant the idea of representation or indeed any other understanding of atonement but simply to argue that substitution is also an important element.) The present chapter will examine what I regard as three of the most intellectually compelling explanations of nonsubstitutionary approaches to the atonement from a spread of international views—one German, one British, one predominantly North American. In addition to being intellectually stimulating, they also seek to take the Pauline epistles seriously. As we proceed, these approaches will be explained and their strengths and (particularly) weaknesses highlighted (1–3). Thereafter, finally, I will draw attention to a common weakness (4).

1. The Tübingen Understanding of Representative "Place-Taking"[2]

The first option is popular in certain quarters in Germany but little understood outside.[3] This approach sees the sacrifices in

2. See, e.g., H. Gese, "The Atonement," in *Essays on Biblical Theology* (Minneapolis: Augsburg, 1981), 93–116; O. Hofius, "Erwägungen zur Gestalt und Herkunft des paulinischen Versöhnungsgedankens," *ZTK* 77 (1980): 186–99, reprinted in Hofius, *Paulusstudien*, WUNT (Tübingen: Mohr, 1989), 1–14; Hofius, "'Gott hat unter uns aufgerichtet das Wort von der Versöhnung' (2 Kor 5, 19)," *ZNW* 71 (1980): 3–20, reprinted in Hofius, *Paulusstudien*, 3–20; Hofius, "Sühne und Versöhnung: Zum paulinischen Verständnis des Kreuzestodes Jesu," in *Paulusstudien*, 33–49; Hofius, "The Fourth Servant Song in the New Testament Letters," in *The Suffering Servant: Isaiah 53 in Jewish and Christian Sources*, ed. B. Janowski and P. Stuhlmacher, trans. D. P. Bailey (Grand Rapids: Eerdmans, 2004), 163–88, esp. 175–83 on Paul.
3. A notable exception that has been helpful in mediating the Tübingen view to an Anglo-American audience is R. H. Bell. See especially his "Sacrifice and Christology in Paul," *JTS* 53 (2002): 1–27, and *Deliver Us from Evil: Interpreting the Redemption from the Power of Satan in New Testament Theology* (Tübingen: Mohr Siebeck, 2007), 190–200 on the Old Testament background (with some helpful criticisms of Gese), and 200–211 on Paul.

Leviticus, especially the prescriptions in chapters 4–5 and for the Day of Atonement in chapter 16, as the key to understanding both the Old Testament theology of atonement and Paul's statements about the death of Christ.

The architect of this approach to atonement is the former Tübingen professor of Old Testament Hartmut Gese. For Gese and his school, atonement takes place not through *substitution* but through a special kind of identification.[4] There is a specific plight that is being addressed in the atoning sacrifice. The plight is that the Israelite's life is forfeit, and so he or she must be willing (symbolically at least) to die.[5] The problem is not so much individual transgressions but that the Israelite needs to be rescued from death. The same is true not just of the individual but also of the nation as a whole.

The solution lies in the sin offering: here, the priest offers an animal on behalf of the sinner to make atonement.[6] Gese focuses at some length on how this atonement comes about. We can see first the mechanism and then the symbolic significance. In the mechanics of the sin offering, the priest (at least in Leviticus 16) takes a bull and two goats: one goat is dispatched as a "scapegoat," whereas the other goat and the bull are slaughtered and their blood sprinkled on the mercy seat inside the Holy of Holies. The bull is the sin offering made for Aaron and his household; the sacrificial goat is slaughtered for (the rest of) the nation. Gese comments that here "two procedures are essential to the cultic process of atonement—(1) the laying on of hands and (2) the blood ritual."[7] We can examine the significance of these two procedures in turn and the intermediate step of the slaughter of the animal, which is also very important.

4. He also rejects the idea of a satisfaction (Gese, "Atonement," 93) and of an atonement concerned with "forgiveness of sins and errors that can be made good" (ibid., 99).
5. Ibid., 99.
6. Except in the provision in Lev. 5:11–13.
7. Gese, "Atonement," 104. Numbering added.

Beginning with (1) the laying on of hands, Gese emphasizes that the point of the priest laying hands on the animal is *not* that sins are *transferred* to the sacrificial animals; rather, by laying hands on the animal the priest *identifies with it*: the imposition of hands creates a "delegated succession" or identification, not a substitution.[8] The animal is inseparably conjoined to the priest, and atonement is therefore made for the *whole* person and indeed for the whole nation (it does not just deal with "sins").[9] What happens on this line of interpretation is that the laying on of hands establishes a connection between the human being and the animal, and so when the animal goes through death, it symbolically takes the person to death with it.

This death of the animal (between 1 and 2) is necessary for two reasons. Initially, in the death of the animal, the people symbolically enter into the judgment of death. The animal does not switch places with the offerer—it does not die instead of the priest or the people as a substitute. Having forfeited life, the people cannot simply escape death; they must pass through it. This is the significance of the death in itself. It also is preliminary to the blood ritual.

Thereafter comes the second key element in Gese's account, (2) the blood ritual. Here, the animal—through its blood—symbolically takes the people with it into the Holy of Holies and thereby into connection with God. The sacrificial animal therefore does not *displace* the offerer but through its death takes the offerer into the Holy of Holies, through judgment, and into contact with God. Negatively, the death is giving up one's life; positively, the blood manipulation means salvific atonement. When the blood of the animal is sprinkled on the mercy seat in the Holy of Holies, the priest and people are connected and reconciled to God through the blood.

8. Ibid., 106.
9. See the emphasis on atonement for the *whole* (i.e., not just the person's detachable sins) in ibid., 106 ("a total substitutionary [i.e., representative] commitment of a life," 115): "It is always the whole that is atoned for."

The sequence of connections in Leviticus 16 is as follows:

PEOPLE → PRIEST → ANIMAL
                → slaughter →
                   BLOOD → HOLY OF HOLIES → GOD

Therefore,

- the *people* as a whole are represented by the *priest*;
- the *priest* establishes a connection with the *animal* by laying hands on it;
- the *animal* therefore carries the identity of the *priest* (and so of the people as a whole);
- the sacrifice of the animal enacts the human forfeiting of life;
- the life of the *animal* (and therefore of *priest* and *people*) is carried in the *blood*;
- the *blood* is sprinkled in the *Holy of Holies*;
- the *blood* thereby comes into contact with *God*;
- ergo, since the blood of the animal comes into contact with *God*, so do the priest and the people, whose identity is carried by the animal.

As Gese sums up the process, "in the *inclusive* place-taking by means of atoning sacrifice, this ritual brings Israel into contact with God."[10]

The principal scholar to apply this to the New Testament is Otfried Hofius. In his first article of a trilogy on reconciliation in Paul, Hofius emphasizes some negatives: reconciliation is of people

---

10. Ibid., 106, emphasis mine. I have also replaced the language of "inclusive substitution" in Crim's translation with that of "inclusive place-taking" instead. The German *Stellvertretung* is ambiguous, but in Gese and Hofius (at least in their positive statements) it does not refer to substitution in the conventional English sense. So, rightly, Bell, *Deliver Us from Evil*. I am particularly grateful to Daniel P. Bailey for first pointing this out to me. See his influential essay "Concepts of *Stellvertretung* in the Interpretation of Isaiah 53," in *Jesus and the Suffering Servant: Isaiah 53 and Christian Origins*, ed. W. H. Bellinger and W. R. Farmer (Harrisburg, PA: Trinity, 1998), 223–50.

to God, not God to people (hence, there is no propitiation).[11] He comes extremely close to advocating a substitution, speaking of God reckoning the transgressions of sinners to the sinless Christ (thus there is a role for the forgiveness of sins)[12] and even referring with approval to the idea of an "exchange."[13] On the other hand, it becomes clear that the place-taking in view is an "*inclusive* place-taking," whereby people come to God *through* the judgment of death (i.e., not by avoiding it).[14] In a second article he gives greater attention to the place of forgiveness, dealing with the clause "not counting people's sins against them" in 2 Corinthians 5:19.[15] He initially quotes with approval a statement of Schlatter that reconciliation takes place through God's forgiving.[16] He immediately qualifies it, however, by saying that one must add that, for Paul, forgiveness is a *consequence* of reconciliation.[17] (Making forgiveness a precondition of reconciliation would presumably make that forgiveness too much like changing divine hostility to divine favor, which Hofius is keen to avoid.)[18] In both articles, the influence of Gese's article on atonement is acknowledged.[19]

Hofius offers a fuller account of the relevance of Gese's theory to the death of Christ in his article "Atonement and Reconciliation."[20]

11. Hofius, "Erwägungen," 188. Page references to this article are to those of the original *ZTK* publication.

12. Ibid., 190: "Das [i.e., God reconciling his enemies] aber geschah dadurch, dass er die Übertretungen der Sünder dem sündlosen Christus anrechnete und ihn stellvertretend für die Schuldigen die Folge ihrer Sünde, das Todesgericht, treffen liess." On forgiveness, see further p. 188.

13. Ibid., 190: "Tausch."

14. Ibid.

15. Hofius, "Gott hat unter uns aufgerichtet das Wort von der Versöhnung"; page numbers here are those of original *ZNW* publication. The chronology of the articles is evident from the ordering in *Paulusstudien* and also from indications within the two articles. See "Erwägungen," 191n6, and "Gott hat unter uns aufgerichtet das Wort von der Versöhnung," 4n7.

16. Hofius, "Gott hat unter uns aufgerichtet das Wort von der Versöhnung," 9.

17. Ibid.

18. See the comments on propitiation above.

19. Hofius, "Erwägungen," 190n5; "Gott hat unter uns aufgerichtet das Wort von der Versöhnung," 9n29.

20. Hofius, "Sühne und Versöhnung." References are to the edition in *Paulusstudien*.

As in Gese's Old Testament, so in Hofius's Paul, the cross is not about satisfaction or propitiation but "corresponds in its essential elements to the Old Testament understanding of cultic atonement, as seen in the priestly theology."[21]

Like the sacrificial animal, Christ includes in his death the whole person—the whole sinner—not just the person's sins.[22] This is because sin is not merely or primarily about actions and deeds but about a corruption at the core of the human person.[23] Jesus's atoning death, therefore, does not so much separate the sinners from their sins as it includes the sinful person in his or her entirety. This is necessary because—on this line of thinking—a person's sins are not merely detachable; sin as a power is an aspect of one's very being. It is unthinkable for Paul that sin could simply be removed or detached from a person—such a thing would mean the detachment of the person from that person's self![24] This understanding of sin follows the view of Kant that guilt is nontransferable because it is internal to the human person. The solution must correspond to such a plight. As Bell has summed up this view, "the only way to deal with sin is therefore to deal with the sinner himself."[25]

Hofius therefore contrasts Gese's "inclusive place-taking" with "exclusive place-taking" (i.e., substitution). The problem with the latter is that it sees atonement primarily as a separation of the sinner from the sins, an act of sin removal whereby sins are transferred to a substitutionary sin bearer.[26] There is a grain of truth in this, Hofius concedes, but it only happens as a consequence of a much more profound *inclusive place-taking*.[27] The principal need is for atonement to deal with sin as a whole. Sin inevitably leads to the judgment of death, and so what is necessary—again, as in

21. Ibid., 44. See also pp. 48–49 for Paul's modifications to the priestly conception, however, in the light of Christ.
22. Ibid., 44.
23. Ibid.
24. Ibid.
25. Bell, *Deliver Us from Evil*, 192.
26. Hofius, "Sühne und Versöhnung," 41.
27. Ibid.

Gese—for a person to be snatched from death is to *pass through* death and come out the other side.[28]

As in the case of the Old Testament sacrifice, therefore, when Christ dies, all die with him (2 Cor. 5:14–21). In Christ the sinner comes to God by passing through the judgment of death and then—freed from that sin and death—to resurrection in new creation. Having passed through this judgment of death, the sinner is united with and reconciled to God. As Hofius puts it in a later article, "Christ has not simply come alongside the sinner in order to take away something—namely, guilt and sin; he has rather become identical with the sinner, in order through the surrender of his life to lead sinners into union with God and thus open to them fellowship with God for the first time."[29]

1.1. Evaluation of the Tübingen View

There is not space here to deal in detail with every aspect of the interpretation of Leviticus or with the theological presuppositions of the Tübingen approach. On the one hand, there is much to admire. The discussions of both Old and New Testaments in this paradigm provide a rich biblical theology of atonement. Gese's account of blood manipulation does justice to the text in ways that many conventional explanations do not. Hofius's discussion gives a helpful account of Christ's representative passing through the judgment of death in places such as Paul's statement that "one died for all, therefore all died" (2 Cor. 5:14). (It is thus no merely therapeutic version of the atonement that anemically tries to avoid talk of divine judgment.)[30] There are, on the other hand, some difficulties that need to be mentioned.

First, Gese lays such stress on the laying on of hands for the atonement ritual that it is strange—if the act of identification is

---

28. Ibid., 42.
29. Hofius, "Fourth Servant Song," 174.
30. This is not meant to imply that the other two models discussed in this chapter are merely therapeutic models!

so important—that the imposition of hands is not mentioned in Leviticus 16 in connection with the sacrificed bull and goat on the Day of Atonement. It does appear in Leviticus 4 and later in 2 Chronicles 29 (but this latter is a special ceremony).[31] In Leviticus 16, the details of the ritual specify the laying of hands on the "scapegoat" but *not* on the slaughtered goat and bull. Dunn rightly notes that it is only in the account of the scapegoat in Leviticus where the significance of the laying on of hands is actually explained.[32]

Second, while the precise function of the bull and the goat that are killed is quite difficult to work out in Leviticus 16, it is hard to avoid the conclusion that the *scapegoat* ("the live goat") *is* a substitutionary offering; this is still the case even if the ritual is also understood as an elimination.[33] Here, when Aaron takes the goat,

> he is to lay both hands on the head of the live goat and confess over it all the wickedness and rebellion of the Israelites—all their sins—*and put them on the goat's head*. He shall send the goat away into the desert in the care of a man appointed for the task. *The goat will carry on itself all their sins* to a solitary place. (Lev. 16:21–22)

In light of this, it is difficult to take the line that the Levitical cult has no substitution, even if this is not so apparent in the blood ritual.[34] Gese himself acknowledges that the meaning of the laying of hands here is "unequivocal."[35] It should also be recognized that

31. It involves twenty-eight animals (2 Chron. 29:21), and in it the temple and the people are reconsecrated (29:5, 31); in fact, while the priests make the sin offering (29:24), the king and the whole assembly lay their hands upon the animals (29:23).

32. J. D. G. Dunn, *The Theology of Paul the Apostle* (Grand Rapids: Eerdmans, 1998), 220.

33. Rightly, G. Röhser, *Stellvertretung im Neuen Testament* (Stuttgart: Verlag Katholisches Bibelwerk, 2002), 35–36, though he perhaps limits too narrowly the sense in which the scapegoat is a substitute.

34. A substitutionary function of the slaughtered offerings is by no means clear, *pace* S. Jeffery, M. Ovey, and A. Sach, eds., *Pierced for Our Transgressions: Rediscovering the Glory of Penal Substitution* (Leicester: Apollos, 2007), 46.

35. Gese, "Atonement," 105.

the scapegoat is as much a sin offering as are the bull and goat that are slaughtered (Lev. 16:5).

Third, we have already noted in the introduction above the danger that Kant's view poses for the freedom and mercy of God. Kantian presuppositions—in combination with a particular view of the Old Testament cult—about guilt and personal identity play a strong role in Hofius's account, where it is taken for granted that sins cannot be dealt with in a manner that would leave the sinner alive.

Finally, in its concern to emphasize the power of sin at the core of the person, the Tübingen view downplays the importance of *sins* plural—individual transgressions. Since this is a difficulty common to all three paradigms discussed here, we will return to it at the end of this chapter.

2. Interchange in Christ[36]

Morna Hooker is closely associated with an alternative approach to atonement that considers substitution to be not only un-Pauline but actually something criticized by Paul.[37] She suggests that Paul's conception of the atonement is best summarized in the language of *interchange*.[38] In brief, in this conception of the atonement, it

36. For the main expositions of interchange, see M. D. Hooker, "Interchange in Christ," in *From Adam to Christ* (Cambridge: Cambridge University Press, 1990), 13–25 (with a helpful summary of the general outline in seven points on pp. 22–25). This essay was first published in *JTS* 22 (1971): 349–61; Hooker, "Interchange and Atonement," in *From Adam to Christ*, 26–41. See also her *Not Ashamed of the Gospel* (Carlisle: Paternoster, 1994), 20–46 (chap. 2: "Paul"), and "On Becoming the Righteousness of God: Another Look at 2 Corinthians 5:21," *NovT* 50 (2008): 358–75.

37. In a discussion of 2 Cor. 5:14–15, Hooker notes that while Paul's statement "one has died for all" may seem like a reference to substitution, he goes on to explain that he means to speak of Christ's death in representative terms ("therefore all died"). She adds, moreover, "The reason that he feels it necessary to spell out the significance of Christ's 'death for all' is, I suggest, precisely because the Corinthians are interpreting Christ's death as a crude exchange: he dies, we live, he suffers, we do not. No, insists Paul." M. D. Hooker, "Paul the Pastor: The Relevance of the Gospel," PIBA 31 (2009): 24.

38. Others have also picked up on this language: see, e.g., C. Breytenbach, "The 'For Us' Phrases in Pauline Soteriology: Considering Their Background and Use,"

is not that Jesus swaps places with his people in this death on the cross. Rather, he goes to the place where they are and takes them from there to salvation.

Hooker sums up her theory in the words of Irenaeus: "Christ became what we are, in order that we might become what he is."[39] In Paul's letters, Hooker considers "interchange" to be particularly well illustrated by two statements in 2 Corinthians:

> For you know the grace of our Lord Jesus Christ, that though he was rich, yet for your sake he became poor, so that you through his poverty might become rich. (2 Cor. 8:9)

> God made him who had no sin to be sin for us, so that in him we might become the righteousness of God. (2 Cor. 5:21)

That is, it is not so much that God made Christ poor and us rich but rather that he entered our poverty in order to bring us out from that poverty in which we exist, to *share* in his riches. Or in the terms of 2 Corinthians 5:21, for Hooker it is not that God switched sinless Christ and sinful humanity but that Christ became sin so that he might deliver us into the status of being righteous before God. Hooker's emphasis is on the fact that *in him* we become the righteousness of God. In short, "Christ identified with the human condition in order that we might be identified with his."[40]

The key elements are as follows:

- The problem of the human condition is sin and death—that is, the sinful condition of Adamic humanity is the position from which people need to be rescued.
- Christ then enters into this condition.

in *Salvation in the New Testament: Perspectives on Soteriology*, ed. J. van der Watt (Leiden: Brill, 2005), 169.

39. Irenaeus, *A.H.* 5, preface, cited in Hooker, "Interchange and Atonement," 26.
40. Hooker, "Interchange and Atonement," 26.

- Christ thereby unites himself to us, but humans also must identify with him.
- Having been united with him in his death, we pass out of death and into resurrection life with him (receiving the declaration "not guilty" as he did).
- We now continue to live with him, and in him we are formed increasingly into his likeness.

To quote a more expansive definition of Hooker's:

> The idea of "interchange" between the believer and Christ is linked with Paul's understanding of the solidarity of mankind with Christ and with Adam. Inevitably, therefore, the relation cannot be a mutual one, since the believer is always dependent upon Christ. Christ identifies himself with the human situation, and shares human experience, even to the point of death; the Christian, however, is able to share Christ's resurrection (and all that this means) only if he is willing to identify himself with Christ's death. By dying with Christ to sin, the believer is able to share in the verdict of "not guilty" pronounced on Christ at the resurrection. The process is a paradoxical one: Christ empties himself and humbles himself in identifying himself with mankind and becoming what men are; they in turn must identify themselves with his shame and death if they are to become what he is in his glorious resurrection life.[41]

Negatively, this is a sharing of experience, not a substitution.

> The interchange of experience is not a straightforward exchange, for we become the righteousness of God *in him*.[42]

If Christ shares our death, it is in order that we might share his resurrection life. Paul's understanding of the process is therefore one of participation, not substitution; it is a sharing of experience,

41. Ibid., 40.
42. Hooker, "Interchange in Christ," 17.*

not an exchange. Christ is identified with us in order that—in him—we might share in what he is.[43]

Hence, despite some superficial similarities, substitution and interchange are quite different.

2.1. Evaluation of Interchange

There are certainly some elements of truth here. In particular, Hooker's account rightly emphasizes that union and participation are integral to some of Paul's key statements, especially perhaps 2 Corinthians 5:21 and 8:9. It ties the incarnation, death, and resurrection of Christ neatly together as all necessary for atonement. (Perhaps in line with the wider commitment to the soteriological significance of the incarnation in English theology, there is more emphasis on the incarnation here than in the Tübingen model and less stress on the cultic background.) Interchange also identifies the tight connection between atonement and ethics in Paul's letters. There are also some difficulties, however.

First, it is far from clear that Paul really *criticizes* a substitutionary view taken by the Corinthians. It seems probable that the Corinthians (as reflected in 1 Corinthians 1–2) and the superapostles of 2 Corinthians did not sufficiently appreciate the cross. The specifics of what that misunderstanding was, however, elude us.

Second, another possible difficulty with the interchange model is that it may not sufficiently account for what is achieved by the *death* of Christ. The death of Christ is important for various reasons: it is the means by which Jesus identifies with the plight of sinful humanity, and it is important as part of the template for Paul's ethics. It also in some sense brings an end to the reign of sin in Adam. It may be, however, that the lack of place for a *positive* role for the cross downplays the position that Paul accords the death of Christ. He can sum up his message as that of "Christ (and him) crucified"

43. Hooker, "Interchange and Atonement," 26–27.

(1 Cor. 1:23; 2:2) and elsewhere refer to the death of Christ as the positive means of salvation (just as he can also do with resurrection). Romans 3:25, the famous passage in which Jesus is described as accomplishing forgiveness "in his blood," is one such example, and there are others (e.g., Rom. 5:6–9; 8:3; Gal. 1:4; 3:13).

Finally, there is again the question of individual sins. The focus in interchange is on the redemption from the Adamic plight of being under sin (singular, perhaps with a capital *S*) and death. As in the Tübingen view, there is little in the way of attention to sins plural, that is, transgressions. We will come back to this point at the end of the chapter.

3. Apocalyptic Deliverance[44]

A third model now gaining currency, particularly in North America, is that of "apocalyptic deliverance."[45] One lucid account of the view is given by J. Louis Martyn in his definition of "cosmological apocalyptic eschatology."

> Anti-God powers have managed to commence their own rule over the world, leading human beings into idolatry and thus into slavery, producing a wrong situation that was not intended by God and that will not be long tolerated by him. For in his own time, God will inaugurate a victorious and liberating apocalyptic war against these evil powers, delivering his elect from their grasp and thus making right that which has gone wrong because of the powers' malignant machinations. This kind of apocalyptic eschatology is fundamental to Paul's letters.[46]

44. For a selection of essays arguing for this position, see especially J. L. Martyn, *Theological Issues in the Letters of Paul* (Edinburgh: T&T Clark, 1997), and some of the contributions to B. Gaventa, ed., *Apocalyptic Paul: Cosmos and Anthropos in Romans 5–8* (Waco: Baylor University Press, 2013).

45. For the purposes of this section, I make no comment on the appropriateness of the term "apocalyptic" to describe the soteriology of Paul; I merely adopt it as the "insider" terminology used by those sketched here.

46. Martyn, *Theological Issues*, 298.

Martyn explicitly contrasts this view (which he holds) with "*fo-rensic* apocalyptic eschatology," which he regards as gravely mistaken. The latter position has "a specific understanding of what is wrong, and a view of the future," as follows:

> Things have gone wrong because human beings have willfully rejected God, thereby bringing about death and the corruption and perversion of the world. Given this self-caused plight, God has graciously provided the cursing and blessing Law as the remedy, thus placing before human beings the Two Ways, the way of death and the way of life. . . . By one's own decision, one can accept God's Law, repent of one's sins, receive nomistic forgiveness, and be assured of eternal life.[47]

Martyn argues, in contrast, that for Paul the plight of humanity does not consist of sins (a "*self-caused* plight") but of enslavement. In Martyn's commentary on Galatians, an individual sin is more characterized as a "misstep" by someone within the church rather than as a key element of the human plight.[48] The human situation is fundamentally one of being subject to hostile cosmic forces and of Christ's invasion of the cosmos to rescue humanity from those forces.

Correspondingly, the solution for Martyn does not consist so much in Christ's sacrificial death for the forgiveness of sins (the view of pre-Pauline tradition and of Paul's *opponents* in Galatians);[49] rather, "human beings are not said to need forgiveness, but rather deliverance from a genuine slavery that involves the Law."[50]

47. Ibid., 299. This is spelled out further especially on pp. 142–44.

48. J. L. Martyn, *Galatians*, Anchor Bible 33A (New Haven: Yale University Press, 1997), 97.

49. See Martyn, *Theological Issues*, 148, where he describes the view of the "teachers" in Galatians as follows: "Jesus's death is the totally adequate sacrifice made by God himself, the sacrifice in which God accomplished the forgiveness of sins for Israel."

50. Ibid., 153. Martyn can also say, however, that Paul may not have given up completely on a sacrificial understanding of the atonement for sins; Paul holds on to the traditional Jewish-Christian understanding of Christ's death (see section 4 on p. 144); for Paul's agreement, see pp. 147–48.

In sum, "the human plight consists fundamentally of enslavement to supra-human powers; and God's redemptive act is his deed of liberation."[51]

It is instructive to observe the ways in which apocalyptically minded interpreters interpret Galatians 1:4 with its reference to Christ "who gave himself for our sins, in order to deliver us from the present evil age." Here, de Boer's commentary on Galatians 1:4 emphasizes that Christ "gave himself for our sins," not to effect forgiveness but "to deliver us from the present evil age."[52] For Martyn, Galatians 1:4a is "a quotation from an early Christian liturgy, a fragment of a confession in which the human plight is identified as 'our sins,' and Christ's death is seen as the sacrificial atonement by which God has addressed that plight."[53] Although Paul might not explicitly disagree with the fragment, verse 4a is not merely an innocent formula. Martyn comments on the possible use of Galatians 1:4a in "the worship services now being conducted in their churches by the Teachers."[54] In Martyn's account of the verse, the apocalyptic note of deliverance is introduced to "correct" the Jewish-Christian formula's reference to Christ giving himself for our sins.[55] This primarily liberative understanding of salvation—as a deliverance from death and Sin (singular with a capital S) rather than atonement for *sins*—has been very influential.[56]

51. Martyn, *Galatians*, 97.

52. M. C. de Boer, *Galatians: A Commentary* (Louisville: Westminster John Knox, 2011), 30.

53. Martyn, *Galatians*, 95.

54. Ibid.

55. Ibid., 90. There is a possible inconsistency in Martyn, however, as later he maintains that Paul does not give up the Jewish-Christian formula (*Galatians*, 269; cf. 273).

56. See, e.g., B. Gaventa, "The Cosmic Power of Sin in Paul's Letter to the Romans: Toward a Widescreen Edition," *Interpretation* 58 (2004): 231: "Sin is Sin—not a lower-case transgression, not even a human disposition or flaw in human nature, but an upper-case Power that enslaves humankind and stands over against God." Cf. also S. G. Eastman, "Apocalypse and Incarnation: The Participatory Logic of Paul's Gospel," in *Apocalyptic and the Future of Theology: With and Beyond J. Louis Martyn*, ed. J. B. Davis and D. Harink (Eugene, OR: Wipf & Stock, 2012), 170: "The human predicament therefore requires more than forgiveness pronounced from on

This account is usually deemed to be incompatible with substitution, and we can see this in remarks that tend to accompany the exegesis of Galatians 3:13: "Christ redeemed us from the curse of the law by becoming a curse for us."[57] Martyn's former student Martinus de Boer expresses clearly one perspective on the logic of why placing liberation at the center of Pauline soteriology leaves little place for substitution. In his comment on Galatians 3:13, he notes that a substitutionary understanding "would imply that Christ took upon himself a penalty that ought to be imposed on human beings."[58] (It is of course a specifically *penal* understanding of substitution targeted here.) The problem with this, he explains, is that human beings are portrayed by Paul as *already* under a curse and are therefore in need of deliverance from a present situation (hence Gal. 1:4) rather than a future plight. Martyn finds the inadequacy of substitution for the apocalyptic model in its limitation of the *dramatis personae* in Galatians to three actors: humanity, God, and Christ as substitutionary mediator. Martyn maintains that what complicates this picture is the addition of "the powerful, enslaving curse of the Law" as a fourth actor: hence, "central to the action in this apocalyptic struggle is, therefore, not forgiveness"—which presumably would have been accomplished by substitution—"but rather victory."[59] In contrast to the drama with three actors, one of which is "Christ as the substitutionary sacrifice," there are four: the introduction of the cosmic power of Sin or the enslaving power of the Law fundamentally changes the landscape and the role of Christ, who (instead?) "comes to embody the enslaving curse."[60] Campbell, following in this line

---

high; it requires a rescue operation on the ground." I owe these references to my former student Joshua Hemmings.

57. For an exception, see Eastman, "Apocalypse and Incarnation," 169–70.

58. De Boer, *Galatians*, 211.

59. Martyn, *Galatians*, 318n110.

60. Martyn (ibid.) talks in terms of Galatians 3:13 being "more than the standard formulation of the doctrine of substitutionary atonement." I am not quite sure of Martyn's attitude to substitution in this footnote; it may be more positive than that of de Boer. Cf. Martyn, *Theological Issues*, 153: "Paul still says that Christ died 'for

of thinking, locates substitution squarely among the evils of the "justification by faith" model of Pauline theology, which is antithetically opposed to the liberative model.[61]

3.1. Evaluation of the Apocalyptic Paradigm

The accounts of Paul given by Martyn and others associated with him in recent times are gripping and useful reminders that Paul's warfare language should be taken seriously, not just as ornamental illustration of something else more fundamental and central. On the other hand, this approach has its weaknesses when the apocalyptic warfare language itself becomes a ruling paradigm governing all the others.

First, this paradigm works well when applied to Galatians, but it has much less explanatory power when applied to Romans—to say nothing of the other letters. (Interpreting 1 Thessalonians along such lines would be a challenge.) Sections of Romans 5–8 can certainly be understood as talking of Christ's deliverance from the reign of sin and death, but such an approach does not work for Romans 1–4. This is graphically illustrated in Campbell's work, where the logical consequence of a panapocalyptic view is to attribute much of Paul's forensic discourse in Romans 1–4 to Paul's rhetorical opponent.[62]

A second, related point is that the characterization of humans as victims in need of rescue from oppressive hostile powers gives only a one-sided account of plight and solution in Paul.[63] Human guilt is a major concern in Romans 1–3, for example, where oppressive

---

us' (Gal. 3:13). But now . . . human beings are not said to need forgiveness, but rather deliverance from a genuine slavery. . . . And by his death, Christ is not said to have accomplished our forgiveness, but rather our redemption from slavery."

61. D. A. Campbell, *The Deliverance of God* (Grand Rapids: Eerdmans, 2009), 33, 185, 325.

62. Ibid., parts 3 and 4.

63. I am grateful for conversations with my student David Shaw on this topic. See now his very helpful analysis in "Apocalyptic and Covenant: Perspectives on Paul or Antinomies at War?," *JSNT* 36 (2013): 155–71.

hostile forces are scarcely to be seen. (The Tübingen approach accounts rather better for human guilt in Paul's writings.) Conversely, in 1 Thessalonians 1, the rescue effected by Jesus is not from diabolical powers but from God's own wrath (cf. also Rom. 5:9). And so on. It might be noted that Colossians 2 seamlessly combines the two: "He forgave us all our transgressions. Having canceled the charge of our debt, with its decrees, which stood against us, he took it away and nailed it to the cross. And having stripped the powers and authorities, he made a public spectacle of them, having triumphed over them by the cross" (Col. 2:13–15).

Third, it is very difficult to identify from the apocalyptic model *how* the death of Christ effects salvation in the form of the liberation described. Apocalyptic accounts of the death of Christ state on a number of occasions that the death of Christ effects the redemption that is the solution to the plight of slavery, but it is hard to find a discussion of how the death of Christ corresponds to this plight and effects the solution envisaged.

Finally, and again relatedly, the general difficulty that we have ascribed to the Tübingen and interchange paradigms applies here also: on the one hand, there is again great emphasis on the enslaving power of Sin, whether thought of as an external cosmic force or as the enemy within; on the other hand, transgressions and trespasses are neglected or at least heavily marginalized. We can now address this point in more detail.

4. The Omission or Downplaying of "Sins"

We have already mentioned the three views here as downplaying sins, that is, individual transgressions. In the Tübingen school they receive short shrift in Gese's account of the Old Testament cult, and in Hofius's account of Paul forgiveness of sins is considered secondary to reconciliation. Hooker's interchange theory also has little place for them. In the apocalyptic model they are relegated to secondary importance at best, considered much more a concern of pre-Pauline tradition and Paul's opponents than of Paul's authentic voice. And this problem of a lack of attention to sins plural is a general difficulty with those approaches to the atonement that make representation or liberation an all-encompassing explanation of the death of Christ.

The problem with such models is that, again, if they are seen as dominant, they neglect a crucial factor in Paul's conception of the atonement, that is, that Paul sees Christ's death as dealing with *sins* plural. *Sins*—individual infractions of the divine will—are frequently mentioned in Paul, and yet one finds them frequently marginalized in scholarship. Two common reasons are given for relativizing their significance.

4.1. "Sins" Infrequent and Uncharacteristic of Paul?

First, then, is the charge that Paul's lack of interest in individual infractions of the divine will is evident from the lack of frequency of "sins" (*hamartiai*) in the plural; characteristic of Paul is, rather, the singular "sin" (or "Sin"). For example, one finds references in scholarship to "the more characteristically Pauline singular"[64] and, conversely, statements that "the plural 'your sins' [in 1 Cor. 15:17] is untypical for Paul."[65]

When such a claim is scrutinized, however, it proves extremely vulnerable: as Dunn has noted, the personification of sin is rare outside of Romans, where one frequently finds plural forms of "sin" and "transgression" vocabulary.[66] Two points are relevant here: (a) there are numerous references to plural acts of disobedience in Paul, and (b) in various cases even references in the singular are to individual acts, not to a hostile power of some kind. A selection of the evidence from the undisputed letters is tabulated here, focusing only on general nouns or noun phrases for sins

64. J. D. G. Dunn, *The Theology of Paul's Letter to the Galatians* (Cambridge: Cambridge University Press, 1993), 43.
65. Hofius, "Fourth Servant Song," 180.
66. Dunn, *Theology of Paul the Apostle*, 111.

rather than words referring to immoral acts of a more specific nature (e.g., hypocrisy, flattery, sexual immorality).

Table 1.1. "Sin" and "Sins" in Paul's Writings

	Singular Referring to an Act	Plural
hamartia	Rom. 4:8; 14:23; 2 Cor. 11:7	Rom. 4:7; 7:5; 11:27; 1 Cor. 15:3, 17; Gal. 1:4; 1 Thess. 2:16
hamartēma	1 Cor. 6:18	Rom. 3:25
parabasis	Rom. 2:23; 4:15; 5:14	Gal. 3:19
paraptōma	Rom. 5:15 (*bis*); 5:17, 18, 20; 11:11, 12; Gal. 6:1	Rom. 5:16; 2 Cor. 5:19
parakoē	Rom. 5:19; 2 Cor. 10:6	
anomia		Rom. 4:7
adikia	Rom. 1:18?; 2 Cor. 12:13	
asebeia	Rom. 1:18?	Rom. 11:26
apeitheia	Rom. 11:30	
(to) kakon	Rom. 2:9; 7:19; 12:17 (*bis*); 13:3 (with *ergon*); 13:4 (*bis*); 13:10; 1 Cor. 13:5; 2 Cor. 13:7; 1 Thess. 5:15 (*bis*)	Rom. 1:30; 3:8; 1 Cor. 10:6
ti . . . phaulon	Rom. 9:11	
ta erga tou skotous		Rom. 13:12
ta erga tēs sarkos		Gal. 5:19
hai praxeis tou sōmatos		Rom. 8:13
pan eidos ponērou	1 Thess. 5:22	

In the undisputed letters, then, Paul refers to individual instances of transgressions a great many times.

Notable here are the references to *hamartiai* (plural), normally translated "sins." Of the seven examples there, the instances in Romans 4:7 and 11:27 come in quotations from the Old Testament, but one should not thereby assume that Paul was therefore forced into using the language. In the disputed epistles this plural occurs in Ephesians 2:1; Colossians 1:14; 1 Timothy 5:22, 24; and

2 Timothy 3:6. None of this is particularly surprising given that Paul also uses the cognate noun *hamartēma* as well as the cognate verb *hamartanō* in the sense of committing particular offenses (Rom. 2:12; 3:23; 5:14, 16; 6:15; 1 Cor. 7:28 [*bis*]; 8:12; 15:34). Paul also employs the rare word *proamartanō* in 2 Corinthians 13:2. In addition, he uses (substantivally) the adjective *hamartōlos* five times in the undisputed letters.[67] This cannot easily mean "someone under the dominion of sin"; it rather means "sinner," "one who is characterized by their committing of sins." Other relevant verbs appear, such as *adikeō* (1 Cor. 6:8; 2 Cor. 7:2, 12). It is also striking that a number of these terms appear in soteriological contexts as characterizing the plight addressed by Christ, for example, Romans 3:25; 5:12–21; 11:26; 1 Corinthians 15:3; 2 Corinthians 5:19; and Galatians 1:4.

The prejudice, therefore, that Paul is not interested in sins (plural) or acts of transgression, however expressed, is a mistaken one. As a result, to explicate the atonement overridingly in terms of victory over Sin as a power is one-sided. Paul frequently refers to the human plight in terms of sins, transgressions, and trespasses, and so it is no surprise to see reference to Christ's death as dealing with these—even summarizing his gospel this way.[68]

---

67. See Rom. 3:7; 5:8, 19; Gal. 2:15, 17. Note also 1 Tim. 1:9, 15.

68. Related to this prejudice is Stendahl's argument that Paul is concerned not with forgiveness but with justification. He rightly notes that there are relatively few references to forgiveness in Paul (by comparison with the Gospels and Acts). It is misleading, however, to assert that "the word 'forgiveness' (*aphesis*) and the verb 'to forgive' (*aphienai*) are spectacularly absent from those works of Paul which are authentic and genuinely of his own writing." The apparent tautology here is that he must account both for the disputed epistles and for instances such as Paul's quotation of Psalm 32 in Romans 4—as a quotation, therefore, it is alleged not to be "genuinely of his own writing." Presumably the reference to removal of sins in Romans 11:27 (citing Isa. 59:20) would fall victim to the same stricture. Much less apparently vulnerable, however, must be one passage in which Paul summarizes the essence of his message as follows: "God was in Christ reconciling the world to himself, *not counting people's trespasses against them*" (2 Cor. 5:19). This is clear evidence that Paul is interested in the forgiveness of sins. Stendahl almost draws attention to the oddity of his own position by the way he makes the argument explaining away the reference to forgiveness in Rom. 4:6–8: "In that case poor Paul could not avoid using a verbal

4.2. "Sins" as Characteristic of Pre-Pauline Formulae?

Closely related to this point is the frequent observation that references to Christ dealing with sins are often judged to belong to pre-Pauline formulae that influenced Paul but (at best) were not really at the core of his "mature" thought. As Martyn comments on Christ's giving himself "for our sins" in Galatians 1:4,

> One point is certain: The formula is to a significant degree foreign to Paul's own theology, for it identifies discrete sins as humanity's (in the first instance, Israel's) fundamental liability. . . . Paul, when he is formulating his own view, consistently speaks not of sins, but rather of Sin.[69]

Paul, according to Martyn, may inherit the language of sins, but it is not properly his own: this particular formula in Galatians 1:4a is—as noted in §3 above—"a quotation from an early Christian liturgy."[70] Hence in his translation of Galatians 1:1–5, Martyn places the phrase "who gave up his very life for our sins" in quotation marks, as something Paul is citing.[71]

There are two main difficulties here.[72] First, commentators often pronounce with unerring confidence that a particular phrase is a

---

form, 'were forgiven,' because he had to quote Psalm 32:1 in which it occurs." On all this, see K. Stendahl, *Paul among Jews and Gentiles* (Philadelphia: Fortress, 1976), 23. Stendahl's influential denial of the importance of forgiveness, however, has the consequence of relativizing the importance of what would be forgiven—namely, sins.

69. Martyn, *Galatians*, 90.

70. Ibid., 95.

71. Ibid., 81.

72. The earliest scholarly references I have been able to find to identify Pauline statements about Christ dealing with "sins" as pre-Pauline formulae (outside of 1 Cor. 15) are A. Seeberg, *Der Katechismus der Urchristenheit* (Leipzig: Deichert, 1903), 52 (cf. 67). Seeberg suggests Gal. 1:4 is a pre-Pauline formula like 1 Cor. 15:3 and describes it as "[eine] Stelle, zu deren Tonart die Berücksichtigung einer Formel jedenfalls trefflich passt." J. Weiss, *Der erste Korintherbrief*, KEK (Göttingen: Vandenhoeck & Ruprecht, 1909), 347, makes the same point and adds 1 Thess. 1:10. In *Das Urchristentum* (Göttingen: Vandenhoeck & Ruprecht, 1917), 75, he expands the list to include Romans 4:25 and 1 Thess. 5:10. Seeberg and Weiss appear to have been pioneers, even if not necessarily the first, in identifying pre-Pauline formulae beyond such explicit cases as 1 Cor. 11:23–26 and 15:3–5.

pre-Pauline formula, when often the matter is far from clear. It is hard to see how Martyn can claim that the case of Galatians 1:4 is simply "certain." Indeed, since the reference to "sins" even appears to be invoked (in the citation above) as part of the evidence for a pre-Pauline formula, the process is worryingly circular. The same applies to other passages, such as Romans 3:25–26 and 4:25.[73]

A second difficulty with this perspective is that it succumbs to the fallacy sometimes found in redaction-critical studies of the Gospels, according to which inherited material is unthinkingly pasted in rather than deliberately absorbed. This is more easily seen in Gospels study, as, for example, in Strecker's comment on Mark 10:45: "This [the atonement], however, is not a genuine Markan idea. Here a sharp distinction must be made between tradition and redaction, since the concept of the atoning death of Jesus belongs to the pre-Markan tradition, as can be seen from the two most important examples in Mark."[74] The difficulty here should be self-evident: why is material actively taken over by Mark not really Markan? As Stanton notes, it was a difficulty in some older redaction-critical approaches that "little or no attention was given to traditions the evangelists retained without modification."[75] (Stanton identifies this as a feature of the first phase of redaction criticism, which was then succeeded by a more balanced second phase.)[76] Pauline scholarship can also view traditional material as not really authentically Pauline, but the same criticism applies as in Gospels study: such an approach treats Paul as an unintelligent scissors-and-paste man.

---

73. The presence of *hamartēma* as suggestive of a non-Pauline origin of Rom. 3:25 (in a Jewish-Christian tradition) is found in E. Käsemann, "Zum Verständnis von Römer 3,24–26," *ZNW* 43 (1950–51): 150; cf. also E. Lohse, *Märtyrer und Gottesknecht: Untersuchungen zur urchristlichen Verkündigung vom Sühntod Jesu Christi* (Göttingen: Vandenhoeck & Ruprecht, 1963), 150. R. Bultmann, *Theologie des Neuen Testaments* (Tübingen: Mohr, 1953), 47, cites both Rom. 3:25 and 4:25 as containing the pre-Pauline idea that Christ deals with sins, identifying 4:25 as formulaic.

74. G. Strecker, *Theology of the New Testament* (Louisville: Westminster John Knox, 2000), 362.

75. G. N. Stanton, *The Gospels and Jesus*, 2nd ed. (Oxford: Oxford University Press, 2002), 29.

76. Ibid., 29–30.

Ziesler's comment on the alleged pre-Pauline formula in Romans 1:3–4 is worth applying here: "Even if he is quoting, it ought to be added, he means what he says."[77]

It is certainly true that Paul refers to "sins" in at least one place where he is citing pre-Pauline tradition: in 1 Corinthians 15:3, the gospel that Christ died for sins is a gospel that is not unique to Paul—it is the gospel that he "received." However, Paul includes this reference to sins in a formula that he says sums up the gospel that is "of first importance." Again, he can sum up his "ministry of reconciliation" from God as announcing "that God was in Christ reconciling the world to himself, *not counting people's sins against them*" (2 Cor. 5:18–19). Downgrading the importance of individual infractions of the divine will, therefore, does not do justice to their importance in Paul's account of the human plight.

5. Conclusion

In this first chapter, I have attempted to expound what I regard as three of the best "competitors" of substitutionary atonement. Analysis of them shows up a number of strengths. The Tübingen view and the interchange model share in common the idea that Christ's death is most fundamentally one of Christ's identification with us. To that extent, they do ample justice to that strand of Paul's thinking. Similarly, the apocalyptic model, with its focus on "Christus Victor" triumphing over the powers in his death and resurrection, also helpfully emphasizes a different aspect of the cross.[78]

Despite the merits of these three, they each have their own problems as well as a problem in common. This is the downplaying of

---

77. J. A. Ziesler, *Paul's Letter to the Romans* (London: SCM, 1989), 60.

78. "Christus Victor" is the title of Gustav Aulén's famous work championing the idea of Christ's conquest of hostile powers as a model of the atonement preferable to the "Latin" view of Anselm and the exemplarist understanding of Abelard. The English version, *Christus Victor: An Historical Study of the Three Main Types of the Idea of the Atonement* (London: SPCK, 1931), was translated from the Swedish edition first published in 1930.

"sins." It is a feature of representative understandings of the atonement that they are more corporate in nature. They are therefore not necessarily particularly well equipped to incorporate reference to that aspect of the human plight that consists of human sins. In a different way, apocalyptic construals of Paul's theology see the plight as consisting in the enslavement of humanity, not its guilt. *Sins*, transgressions, individual infractions of the divine will are, however, integral to Paul's account of humanity's plight.

A methodological problem is also evident in varying degrees in these three accounts. That is, they adopt a particular view of the atonement in Paul, and this theory tends to take on the role of a dominant or all-encompassing explanation: in consequence, with such a model becoming an organizing framework, it can be used as a criterion for whether other elements may or may not be fitted into Paul. A difficulty in these three accounts thus arises in part out of wanting to make a single paradigm fit Paul's references to the atonement across the board. It is of course a worthy pursuit to want to discover a single elegant theory that takes account of all the data, but this should not lead to a Procrustean neglect of the more substitutionary passages.

More flexibly, Dunn has remarked that accounts of the cross in Paul need to incorporate a variety of perspectives. He lists "representation, sacrifice, curse, redemption, reconciliation, conquest of the powers."[79] The aim of this book is to add substitution to this list.[80] The next two chapters will look at two particular case studies that, in different ways, testify to Paul's understanding of Christ's death as substitutionary.

---

79. Dunn, *Theology of Paul the Apostle*, 231.

80. Dunn, with some significant reservations, accepts substitution as a component of Paul's theology of the cross. See J. D. G. Dunn, "Paul's Understanding of the Death of Jesus as Sacrifice," in *Sacrifice and Redemption: Durham Essays in Theology*, ed. S. W. Sykes (Cambridge: Cambridge University Press, 1991), 51: "Although 'substitution' expresses an important aspect of Paul's theology of the atonement, I am not sure that Paul would have been happy with it or that it is the best single word to serve as the key definition of that theology."

2

"Christ Died for Our Sins according to the Scriptures" (1 Cor. 15:3)

Chapter 1 was primarily concerned with discussing three possible views of the atonement in Paul, views that have been offered as alternatives to substitution. The aim of chapters 2 and 3 is to show not that these approaches are totally wrong but that they are mistaken in denying substitution. These chapters hope to make a positive case for substitution by way of two case studies, 1 Corinthians 15:3 and Romans 5:6–8. These two chapters look at two different interpretations of the death of Christ: that he "died for our sins" and that he "died for us." As Christina Eschner has emphasized, "dying for sins" and "dying for us" are not simply two variant forms of the same thing but rather have different meanings.[1] The present chapter is a study of the former.

1. C. Eschner, *Gestorben und hingegeben „für" die Sünder: Die griechische Konzeption des Unheil abwendenden Sterbens und deren paulinische Aufnahme für die*

It was noted in the previous chapter that one of the failures common to each of the three theories discussed was a failure to account for *sins* (plural), discrete infractions of the divine will. This chapter draws attention to a passage where Paul explicitly says that Christ's death deals with sins:

> Now, brothers and sisters, I want to remind you of the gospel I preached to you, which you received and on which you have taken your stand. By this gospel you are saved, if you hold firmly to the word I preached to you. Otherwise, you have believed in vain.
>
> For what I received I passed on to you as of first importance: that *Christ died for our sins according to the Scriptures*, that he was buried, that he was raised on the third day according to the Scriptures, and that he appeared to Cephas, and then to the Twelve. After that, he appeared to more than five hundred of the brothers and sisters at the same time, most of whom are still living, though some have fallen asleep. Then he appeared to James, then to all the apostles, and last of all he appeared to me also, as to one abnormally born.
>
> For I am the least of the apostles and do not even deserve to be called an apostle, because I persecuted the church of God. But by the grace of God I am what I am, and his grace to me was not without effect. No, I worked harder than all of them—yet not I, but the grace of God that was with me. Whether, then, it is I or they, this is what we preach, and this is what you believed. (1 Cor. 15:1–11)

The aim of this chapter, then, is to examine Paul's theology of the atonement through the lens of the words "Christ died for our

---

Deutung des Todes Jesu Christi (Neukirchen-Vluyn: Neukirchener Verlag, 2010), 357; similarly C. Breytenbach, "'For Us' Phrases in Pauline Soteriology: Considering Their Background and Use," in J. van der Watt, ed., *Salvation in the New Testament: Perspectives on Soteriology* (Leiden: Brill, 2005), 173. See, by contrast, e.g., R. Bieringer, "Traditionsgeschichtlicher Ursprung und theologische Bedeutung der ὑπέρ-Aussagen im Neuen Testament," in *The Four Gospels 1992: Festschrift Franz Neirynck*, ed. F. van Segbroeck, C. M. Tuckett, G. van Belle, and J. Verheyden (Leuven: Leuven University Press/Peeters, 1992), 1:223, 238, for an expression of the essential similarity of the "long" and "short" forms of the "dying formula."

sins according to the Scriptures" (1 Cor. 15:3). In the course of it, we will observe three points. First, we will justify the *primary importance* of the gospel, of which a central component for Paul is Christ's death "for our sins." Second, as background to Paul's statement, we will explore *which* Scriptures Paul had in mind when he described his gospel as "according to the Scriptures." Finally, the third part will draw attention to the substitutionary content of the death of Christ in 1 Corinthians 15:3.

1. The Importance of 1 Corinthians 15:3–4

The crucial importance of 1 Corinthians 15:3–4 for our understanding of the Pauline gospel must surely not be underplayed. It is perhaps more natural to think of Romans as the most convenient place to look for an exposition of the gospel, perhaps with a convenient summary in Romans 1:16–17: "I am not ashamed of the gospel, because it is the power of God for the salvation of everyone who believes: first for the Jew, then for the Gentile. For in the gospel the righteousness of God is revealed, from faith to faith, just as it is written: 'The righteous will live by faith.'" But 1 Corinthians 15:3–4 might have just as good a claim (if not better) than Romans 1:16–17 to be a distillation of the gospel. Romans aside, we can at least see the importance of the 1 Corinthians summary through a sketch of the language with which Paul frames his statements about the cross and resurrection there.

Verse 1. "*Now, brothers and sisters, I want to remind you of the gospel I preached to you.*" Here Paul recollects for the Corinthians what he has already told them, the gospel that he preached to them when he was in Corinth. This gospel was not merely an event or happening that was in some way related to Paul's preaching; it was the actual verbal content of that preaching, which is why he can now recount it. Paul is saying here that 1 Corinthians 15:3–4 (or 3–5) *is* the gospel, at least in brief summary form.

Verse 2. "Through which you were saved." As the gospel, it is the means by which the Corinthians are saved, as per Romans 1:16–17: the gospel is God's saving power for all who believe. Salvation is a centrally important factor for Paul, and so the message by which that salvation takes place is important as well.

Verse 3. "As of first importance." It is a minor matter of scholarly debate whether this indicates that the gospel is what Paul communicated to the Corinthians first in time, or whether he preached about its primary significance.[2] Either way, it amounts to the same thing: what he is reminding them about the gospel in the letter here is captured in many translations—it is "of first importance" (NIV, NRSV, ESV).

Verse 11. "Whether, then, it is I or they, this is what we preach." This Pauline gospel is not the proclamation of a maverick apostle who goes his own way, ignoring what the other apostles do. Paul makes it clear in verse 11 that this gospel of his is the same as that preached by the other apostles: "so whether it is I or they, this is what we preach, and this is what you believed." This is a significant and oft-neglected passage. As Hengel and Schwemer put it, 1 Corinthians 15:11 is "a text which scholars are persistently fond of suppressing. . . . Nevertheless, . . . precisely because Paul was such a contentious theologian, 1 Corinthians 15:11 is a tremendous statement to come from his pen."[3] What we will see as the substitutionary death and resurrection of Christ according to the Scriptures as Paul spells it out in 1 Corinthians 15:3–4 is thus not the peculiar eccentricity of an apostolic lone ranger but the proclamation of the whole apostolic college.

So in a "quest for Paul's gospel"—and indeed, for the apostolic gospel—why not start with 1 Corinthians 15? It seems odd to

---

2. A. C. Thiselton, *The First Epistle to the Corinthians*, NIGTC (Carlisle: Paternoster, 2000), 1186.

3. M. Hengel and A. M. Schwemer, *Paul between Damascus and Antioch* (London: SCM, 1997), 290, 291.

me that a 2005 monograph by Douglas Campbell, *The Quest for Paul's Gospel*, has scarcely any discussion of the passage. Among the three references to 1 Corinthians 15:3–4, one notes that the atoning death of Christ apparently occupies a "marginal role."[4] I merely mention Campbell as one example of a wider tendency, but we have seen some of the difficulties in the previous chapter with construing Paul's soteriology in a way that neglects how the death of Jesus deals with particular infractions of God's will (among other things). Campbell also remarks that Christ's death is "mentioned briefly" in the passage and so for this reason perhaps is not very significant.[5] But the reason it is mentioned briefly is that Paul is expressing the gospel in summary or shorthand form. The brevity of Paul's statements here does nothing to relativize their primary importance.[6]

In the framing of Paul's statements in 1 Corinthians 15:3–4 in their wider setting in verses 1–11, then, we see how significant the death of Christ for our sins is according to Paul. We move to explore what Paul meant when he wrote that Jesus's death is in accordance with the Scriptures.

2. "According to the Scriptures"

Scholars have proposed a number of possible explanations for why Paul says that Christ's death and resurrection on the third day each

---

4. D. A. Campbell, *The Quest for Paul's Gospel: A Suggested Strategy* (New York: Continuum, 2005), 198.

5. Ibid., 183.

6. M. D. Hooker does greater justice to the gospel summary in 1 Corinthians 15, although it does not feature at all in the interchange essays. In *A Preface to Paul* (New York: Oxford University Press, 1980), 21–22, it is a jumping-off point for discussing the death and resurrection of Christ as the core facts of the gospel, but this fact of the death is understood as interpreted by Paul (in the following chapter) primarily (though not exclusively) as an incorporative interchange. Similarly in Hooker's *Not Ashamed of the Gospel: New Testament Interpretations of the Death of Christ* (Carlisle: Paternoster, 1994), 20–46, the formula in 1 Cor. 15:3 is mentioned as a starting point but not explained.

take place "according to the Scriptures." One explanation is that it is not specific Old Testament passages that Paul has in mind.[7] It could be that Paul refers to a general pattern in the Old Testament in which God makes Israel as well as individuals go through exile, misery, and even death before displaying his glory through saving them. The overarching pattern of Israel's history—sin, exile, return—is one case in point. Within that larger framework, the life story of Joseph is another. The pattern is neatly and poetically expressed in Hannah's Song:

> The LORD brings death and makes alive;
>   he brings down to the grave and raises up.
> The LORD sends poverty and wealth;
>   he humbles and he exalts. (1 Sam. 2:6–7)

The theme is thus part of the warp and woof of the Old Testament, and so one might not need to posit a particular passage as the background to Paul's death/resurrection statement.

On the other hand, there is not really a shortage of specific passages as candidates. For the resurrection on the third day, there is the Old Testament "type" of Jonah, already used by Jesus:

> For as Jonah was three days and three nights in the belly of a huge fish, so the Son of Man will be three days and three nights in the heart of the earth. (Matt. 12:40)

Even closer to Paul's resurrection language in 1 Corinthians 15:4 is Hosea 6:[8]

---

7. Thus A. Eriksson, *Traditions as Rhetorical Proof: Pauline Argumentation in I Corinthians* (Stockholm: Almquist & Wiksell, 1998), 93; Eschner, *Gestorben und hingegeben*, 111.

8. The parallels between Paul and the Greek of Hosea 6:2 are especially striking. Cf. Paul's *egēgertai tēi hēmerāi tēi tritēi* and LXX Hosea: *en tēi hēmerāi tēi tritēi anastēsometha kai zēsometha enōpion autou* (Hos. 6:2). The last clause here also may be echoed in Paul: see, e.g., Rom. 6:8 (*suzēsomen autōi*) and 1 Thess. 5:10 (*hama sun autōi zēsōmen*).

> Come, let us return to the LORD.
> He has torn us to pieces
>> but he will heal us;
> he has injured us
>> but he will bind up our wounds.
> After two days he will revive us;
>> on the third day he will restore us [Greek: we will rise],
>> that we may live in his presence. (Hos. 6:1–2)

These passages are both possible reasons why Paul might say that resurrection on the third day is according to the Scriptures. But what of Christ's death for sins? As we saw in the previous chapter, for Gese the Levitical cult is the best backdrop. One of the most important ingredients for 1 Corinthians 15:3, however, is Isaiah 53. As we shall see, Paul knows the passage, referring to it elsewhere. The suffering servant, as the only human instance of vicarious death "according to the Scriptures," is the closest model for Christ's death. There are similarities in the structure of the formula as well as in the language of "death" and "sins." (Of course these are only strong similarities, not identities.) Table 2.1 below is intended to highlight the structural and linguistic similarities between 1 Corinthians 15:3 and Isaiah 53, to which we will return. We will also see in §3.2 below that there is an additional but related dimension, namely, the standard Old Testament assumption that sinning leads to death.

2.1. Isaiah 53

An excellent introduction to the study of Isaiah 53 can be found in an essay by the German Old Testament scholar Bernd Janowski entitled "He Bore Our Sins: Isaiah 53 and the Drama of Taking Another's Place," which makes three main points that are relevant here.[9]

---

9. B. Janowski, "He Bore Our Sins: Isaiah 53 and the Drama of Taking Another's Place," in *The Suffering Servant: Isaiah 53 in Jewish and Christian Sources,*

First, chapter 53 must be read within the wider framework of
the surrounding chapters in Isaiah. The people of Israel are hard-
hearted and in a state of disobedience; they refuse to repent and be
gathered by God. They are "deaf" and accused of being "blind"
four times in the space of two verses in chapter 42 (42:18–19; cf.
42:20). Despite having been called as the light to the nations, they
have utterly failed in this vocation. The blindness of Israel is obviously particularly ironic given this calling to be a "light." So there
is the sin of Israel that permeates the whole of this block of Isaiah.

Second, despite this, God undertakes to redeem them. He gives
them words of comfort in chapter 40, he promises in chapter 44
(v. 21) that he has not forgotten Israel, and he even insists that in
the absence of repentance on Israel's part, he will accomplish it
himself (chap. 46).

Third, we see how this will happen. As these chapters (the 40s
and 50s in Isaiah) go on, it becomes clearer that God is raising up
a servant who is *distinct* within the nation: the servant is not just
a way of talking about Israel as a whole but is an individual who
is going to be instrumental in saving the people. This character
is the one who suffers in chapter 53. He is cruelly forsaken by the
nation as a whole, and yet the Israelites later come to realize that
he had accomplished their salvation. Janowski describes the two
stages as follows:

> Prior to the servant's death, Israel wrongly assumed that his suf-
> ferings were the result of his *own* guilt. . . . Hence they kept their
> distance from this "man of sorrows."[10]

Afterward, however,

> They acknowledge the guilt borne by the servant as their own. . . .
> On the one hand they have an insight into the Servant's innocence;

---

ed. B. Janowski and P. Stuhlmacher, trans. D. P. Bailey (Grand Rapids: Eerdmans,
2004), 48–74.

10. Ibid., 48.

on the other they have the insight that their own guilt has been wiped out by the Servant's suffering.[11]

Hence Janowski talks about Isaiah 53 as a "drama of delayed recognition."

2.2. Isaiah 53 in Paul

What, then, could be more natural than for a Jewish Christian such as Paul to see Isaiah 53 as describing the drama of Christ's death? Isaiah describes a prophetic figure who has been rejected and killed. Subsequently, however, people realize that this figure who appeared to have been cursed by God was actually God's chosen savior. The delayed recognition by Israel in Isaiah 53 thus corresponds very well to the delayed recognition by Jewish Christians like Paul himself.

So it may seem natural that Paul might use Isaiah 53, but does he in fact do so? The 1959 monograph of Morna Hooker, *Jesus and the Servant*, replied "no."[12] At the time, this was something of a reaction against a tendency in some scholarly and popular circles to see Isaiah 53 behind every tree. Nearly forty years after the publication of Hooker's volume, a conference was held to discuss the state of the question, and the collected contributions were published in 1998.[13] In this collection, one of the most interesting responses to Hooker's book actually comes from Professor Hooker herself in her comment that she considers that Romans 4:25 is in fact a "clear echo of Isaiah 53" and that it may even have been the case that Paul was first responsible for the connection between Jesus and Isaiah 53.[14] In fact, Romans 4:25 is the most

---

11. Ibid., 70.

12. M. D. Hooker, *Jesus and the Servant: The Influence of the Servant Concept of Deutero-Isaiah in the New Testament* (London: SPCK, 1959).

13. The papers are published as W. H. Bellinger and W. R. Farmer, eds., *Jesus and the Suffering Servant: Isaiah 53 and Christian Origins* (Harrisburg: Trinity, 1998).

14. M. D. Hooker, "Did the Use of Isaiah 53 to Interpret His Mission Begin with Jesus?," in Bellinger and Farmer, *Jesus and the Suffering Servant*, 101, 103.

widely acknowledged parallel to Isaiah 53, with its reference to Jesus "who was handed over for our transgressions." This corresponds in particular to the fact that the servant "was handed over for their sins" (Isa. 53:12).[15] The language is remarkably similar in Paul and the Greek Old Testament at this point. There is virtually a scholarly consensus now that Paul's letters were influenced by Isaiah 53 in their depictions of Jesus's atoning death. To the parallel in Romans 4, one can almost certainly add Romans 8:32 and Isaiah 53:6:[16]

He (God) handed him over for us all. (Rom. 8:32)

All we like sheep have gone astray; man has wandered on his own way. And the LORD has handed him over for our sins. (Isa. 53:6)

Paul, then, has no trouble in using the language of Isaiah 53 to describe Jesus's death.[17]

2.3. Isaiah 53 in 1 Corinthians 15

To get back to the passage that is our main focus, Isaiah 53 also probably lies behind 1 Corinthians 15:3. Three points speak in favor of this. First, there is the hugely strong *prima facie* evidence that the suffering servant in Isaiah 53 is the only case of a human being who dies a vicarious death and thereby deals with the sins of others. Second, there is the structure common to both some of the statements in Isaiah 53 and Paul's formula in 1 Corinthians: in Isaiah, we see instances of he + a verb/phrase of suffering or death + preposition + our misdeeds. This is clear from table 2.1.

---

15. Compare *hos paredothē dia ta paraptōmata hēmōn* (Rom. 4:25a) with *dia tas hamartias autōn paredothē* (Isa. 53:12). The whole of 53:12 has two instances of *paredothē*.

16. Compare *huper hēmōn pantōn paredōken auton* (Rom. 8:32) with Isa. 53:6: *kurios paredōken auton tais hamartiais hēmōn*.

17. According to Nestle-Aland's count, Paul quotes from Isaiah 52 four times: Isa. 52:4, 11 (2 Cor. 6:17); Isa. 52:5 (Rom. 2:24); Isa. 52:7 (Rom. 10:15); Isa. 52:15 (Rom. 15:21); cf. also Isa 53:1 (Rom. 10:16).

Table 2.1

(Word order of Greek deliberately adapted for clarity)

1 Cor. 15:3	Christ	died	for	our	sins
	(Χριστὸς	ἀπέθανεν	ὑπὲρ	ἡμῶν	τῶν ἁμαρτιῶν)
Isa. 52:13	my servant ὁ παῖς μου				
53:4	he οὗτος	bears φέρει		our ἡμῶν	sins τὰς ἁμαρτίας
53:4	he οὗτος	suffers pain ὀδυνᾶται	for περὶ	us ἡμῶν	
53:5	he αὐτὸς	was wounded ἐτραυματίσθη	for διὰ	our ἡμῶν	iniquities τὰς ἀνομίας
	he	was beaten μεμαλάκισται	for διὰ	our ἡμῶν	sins τὰς ἁμαρτίας
	on him ἐπ' αὐτὸν	punishment παιδεία	for our peace εἰρήνης ἡμῶν		
	(by) his αὐτοῦ	stripe τῷ μώλωπι	we were healed ἡμεῖς ἰάθημεν		
53:6	him αὐτὸν	he handed over παρέδωκεν	(for) 	our ἡμῶν	sins ταῖς ἁμαρτίαις
53:7	like a sheep ὡς πρόβατον	led to slaughter ἐπὶ σφαγὴν ἤχθη			
53:8	his life ἡ ζωὴ αὐτοῦ	is taken from the earth αἴρεται ἀπὸ τῆς γῆς			
	he	was led to death ἤχθη εἰς θάνατον	by ἀπὸ	my people's τοῦ λαοῦ μου	iniquities τῶν ἀνομιῶν
53:11	he αὐτὸς	will take up ἀνοίσει		their αὐτῶν	sins τὰς ἁμαρτίας
53:12	his life ἡ ψυχὴ αὐτοῦ	handed over to death παρεδόθη εἰς θάνατον	for(?) ἀνθ'	those . . . ὧν [τῶν ἰσχυρῶν]	
53:12	he αὐτὸς	took up ἀνήνεγκεν		many's πολλῶν	sins ἁμαρτίας
53:12	he	was handed over παρεδόθη	for διὰ	their αὐτῶν	sins τὰς ἁμαρτίας
Rom. 4:25	who ὃς	was handed over παρεδόθη	for διὰ	our ἡμῶν	transgressions τὰ παραπτώματα
Gal. 1:4a	who τοῦ	gave himself δόντος ἑαυτὸν	for ὑπὲρ/περὶ	our ἡμῶν	sins τῶν ἁμαρτιῶν

Third, in terms of specifics, at several points we have reference to the servant's death (the second column in the table): the servant is "led to death" (53:8) and "handed over to death" (53:12). There are also at various points parallels to Paul's phrase "for our sins" (cols. 4–6 in the table). In particular, Greek Isaiah uses the plural of the word *hamartia*—Paul's word for sins in 1 Corinthians 15—six times in chapter 53.

Some have argued against the influence of Isaiah 53 here. It has been objected that Isaiah 53 was not interpreted messianically during the "intertestamental" period, though it is hard to see the force of this objection.[18] It is true that there is little evidence of Second Temple–period Jews seeing Isaiah 53 as a messianic passage (but the question is a complex one).[19] One must give credence to the strong likelihood, however, of innovations by Jesus and the early Christians.[20]

More significant is the objection that the language in the 1 Corinthians tradition is too distant from that of the suffering servant.[21] Specifically, Paul's verb "to die" (*apothnēiskō*) and his preposition

18. It appears perhaps to be made more in response to those who have claimed the opposite rather than as a material objection to arguments for the influence of Isaiah 53 upon the New Testament. See the discussion in S. K. Williams, *Jesus' Death as Saving Event: The Background and Origin of a Concept* (Missoula, MT: Scholars Press, 1975), 111–20.

19. See esp. M. Hengel with the collaboration of D. P. Bailey, "The Effective History of Isaiah 53 in the Pre-Christian Period," in *The Suffering Servant: Isaiah 53 in Jewish and Christian Sources*, ed. B. Janowski and P. Stuhlmacher (Grand Rapids: Eerdmans, 2004), 75–146.

20. M. Hengel, *The Atonement: A Study of the Origins of the Doctrine in the New Testament* (London: SCM, 1981), 57–59.

21. This objection is found in C. Breytenbach, "Jes^LXX 53,6.12 als Interpretatio Graeca und die urchristlichen Hingabeformeln," in *Die Septuaginta: Texte, Theologien, Einflüsse*, ed. W. Kraus and M. Karrer, WUNT 252 (Tübingen: Mohr Siebeck, 2010), 669–70, who comments that very few would emphasize a clear link between Isa. 53 and 1 Cor. 15:3. While one may argue about how clear the link is, there are numerous family resemblances between the two passages, as this chapter sets out. Breytenbach is followed by C. Eschner, "Die Hingabe des einzigen Sohnes ,für'-uns alle: Zur Wiederaufnahme des Sterben-,für'-Motivs aus Röm 5,6–8 in Röm 8,32," in *The Letter to the Romans*, ed. U. Schnelle (Leuven: Leuven University Press/Peeters, 2009), 663; Eschner, *Gestorben und hingegeben*, 111.

"for" (*huper*)[22] are both absent from Isaiah 53. In response, first, on the reference to "dying," although we do not have the verb, we have the cognate noun: in verses 8 and 12, the servant is led away or handed over "to death," and there is a further instance in verse 9, all with the noun *thanatos* ("death," cognate with the verb *apothnēiskō*). Second, the variations in the prepositions are not particularly significant: in Paul one can find Christ dying "for" sins expressed using the Greek prepositions *huper* (as here), *peri* (variant manuscript reading of Gal. 1:4; cf. 1 Thess. 5:10), and *dia* (Rom. 4:25; cf. 1 Cor. 8:11).[23] The prepositions are almost interchangeable. These objections, then, are not sufficient to outweigh the strong, obvious similarity between the figures of Jesus and the servant as well as the similarities in structure and language common to the expressions in Isaiah 53 and 1 Corinthians 15.[24]

The first part of the death-resurrection formula in 1 Corinthians 15:3–4, therefore, is clearly influenced to a large extent by Isaiah 53. (I have no intention in the present study to comment on what may have been the origin of the formula or of the idea of Jesus's vicarious death.) Whoever first delivered this apparently pre-Pauline formula to Paul modeled it at least in part on Isaiah 53.[25] Given that Paul quotes from Isaiah 52 extensively and that

22. I am retaining the older style of transliterating the upsilon with English *u*.

23. In addition to instances in Paul, compare the eucharistic words in Mark 14:24 (with *huper*, or in some manuscripts *peri*) and Matt. 26:28 (with *peri*). See Bieringer, "Traditionsgeschichtlicher Ursprung," 224–25.

24. It is sometimes stated that there is a contrast between sins as the *cause* of the servant's death in Isaiah 53 and Jesus's death in Paul: in the latter case sins are dealt with in the death rather than being the *cause*. See Eschner, "Die Hingabe des einzigen Sohnes," 677–78; Eschner, *Gestorben und hingegeben*, 111. As we will see in §3.2 below, however, the meaning is partly causal in Paul. See also the remarks of H. S. Versnel, "Making Sense of Jesus' Death: The Pagan Contribution," in *Deutungen des Todes Jesu im Neuen Testament*, ed. J. Frey and J. Schröter, WUNT 181 (Tübingen: Mohr Siebeck, 2005), 215–94 (290–91).

25. Scholars have made various suggestions, such as Jerusalem or Antioch, for the provenance of the formula, but the question is not relevant to the present discussion. For Jerusalem, see, e.g., Hengel, *Atonement*, 38; Eriksson, *Traditions as Rhetorical Proof*, 91 (with references to others taking the same view); in contrast, Koester is more skeptical: H. Koester, "The Structure and Criteria of Early Christian Beliefs,"

Isaiah 53 influences Paul's phraseology elsewhere, he would himself have understood this formula in those terms as well.

3. Substitution in 1 Corinthians 15:3

Third, then, we should examine the substitutionary content of Paul's statement. We will see here the relevance again of Isaiah 53 but also the way in which Isaiah 53 modifies a standard assumption in the Old Testament, namely, that sinning leads to one's own death. It is important to grasp both of these elements in order to understand the significance of Christ dying for our sins.

3.1. Substitution in Isaiah 53

To begin with, we can examine substitution in Isaiah 53. Vicariousness—in the sense of exclusive substitution—is clearly present in the Hebrew text.[26] The pronouns are all-important: in particular, there is a "he" who suffers, and he suffers *alone*. The people look back on him as an individual. In addition to the "he," there is also a "we" who are responsible for this suffering and yet are miraculously saved by it.[27] *Death* is there in the Hebrew

in *Trajectories through Early Christianity*, ed. J. M. Robinson and H. Koester (Philadelphia: Fortress, 1971), 226. For discussion, see J. S. Kloppenborg, "An Analysis of the Pre-Pauline Formula 1 Cor 15:3b–5 in Light of Some Recent Literature," *CBQ* 40 (1978): 352–57.

26. Attempts to argue that substitution is not present appeal to a reconstructed historical context of the passage or the wider theological context of the Old Testament rather than (i.e., in contradiction to!) the actual content of Isaiah 53. See, e.g., the objections of Williams, following Snaith and Orlinsky, that (a) the historical context of the exile meant that the nation had not escaped penalty but had, in the exile, endured it, and (b) the legal contract of the covenant simply forbade unjust suffering of one instead of another. See S. K. Williams, *Jesus's Death as Saving Event*, 108–10. It is questionable, however, whether readers in the first century necessarily read Isaiah 53 with the same historical context in mind as do modern Old Testament scholars. In response to the theological-legal objection, the whole tone of Isaiah 53 is one of shocking contrast to the norm. "Who has believed our message?" (Isa. 53:1)—apparently the answer is: not all modern scholars.

27. See D. J. A. Clines, *I, He, We, and They: A Literary Approach to Isaiah 53* (Sheffield: Sheffield Academic Press, 1976).

text—the servant is "cut off from the land of the living" (53:8), led like a lamb to the slaughter (53:7), given a grave with the wicked (53:9) and a place with the rich in his death (53:9), and "handed over to death" (53:12). This death is the *consequence* of wicked persecution by the people: he was despised and rejected by people (53:3); he was oppressed and afflicted (53:7); this cruelty was inflicted because the people considered him divinely cursed—or possibly *vice versa* (53:4). His death, however, is not merely *caused* by the sinful behavior of his persecutors but also regarded as a punishment *in place of* the people for their benefit:

> Surely he took up our pain and bore our suffering, yet we considered him punished by God, stricken by him, and afflicted. But he was pierced for our transgressions, he was crushed for our iniquities; the punishment that brought us peace was on him, and by his wounds we are healed. (Isa. 53:4–5)

The perspective in verse 4 is of the "we" looking back upon themselves, casting their minds back to a time when they looked down from a position of strength upon another ("him") suffering alone. Although they did not realize it at the time, "he" was bearing the afflictions of those who now look back on themselves as having been guilty. The substitutionary character of the death in verse 5 is clear enough: the speakers are alive to tell the tale because they were rescued by the one who died for them and bore their guilt in their place.

Because of the difficulty of the Hebrew in Isaiah 53, the Greek translator, who was probably working in the second century BCE, struggled a little with it. The overall sense is the same, but death is amplified further in the Greek versions: "for the sins of my people he was led away to death" (53:8d).[28] There are, as in the Hebrew, clearly soteriological implications to this death: "discipline for our peace came on him; by his wounds we have been healed" (53:5).

---

28. Hebrew *lamō* ("to him") being read as *lamawet* or *lamōt* ("to death").

The servant in Isaiah 53, then, in both the Hebrew text and the Greek version, is viewed as having undergone a substitutionary death.

3.2. The Converse: Deaths for Sins and Vicarious Death Prohibitions

In general, however, the Old Testament does not say much, and indeed can even be negative, about vicarious death. But there is nevertheless evidence from the Greek Old Testament that the language Paul uses should be understood in this way.

The Old Testament norm is represented by King Zimri—"he died for his sins which he had committed" (1 Kings 16:18–19 LXX: *apethanen huper tōn hamartiōn autou hōn epoiēsen*). The daughters of Zelophehad in Numbers 27 confess, "Our father died in the wilderness. He was not among the company of those who gathered themselves together against the Lord in the company of Korah, but *died for his own sin*" (Num. 27:3: *dia hamartian autou apethanen*). Here, then, Zelophehad perished not in an act of collective judgment by God but rather as an individual. It is the standard view of the Old Testament that people die as a result of their sins. Death is the divine penalty for transgressing; because everybody transgresses, everybody dies. Ezekiel in particular is full of such statements.[29]

Sometimes sin and death are not regarded individualistically, but especially in the case of egregious sin, the judgment spreads more widely than the single sinner. The fate of Achan, to be punished by the people for his notorious offence, came into effect: he, therefore, "died for his own sin" (Josh. 22:20: *apethanen tēi heautou hamartiāi*). Interestingly, however, this judicial death of Achan is combined with the divinely inflicted wrath on Israel, which was

---

29. O. Hofius, "The Fourth Servant Song in the New Testament Letters," in *The Suffering Servant: Isaiah 53 in Jewish and Christian Sources*, ed. B. Janowski and P. Stuhlmacher, trans. D. P. Bailey (Grand Rapids: Eerdmans, 2004), 163–88 (178n63), cites Ezek. 3:18–20; 18:17–18, 24, 26; 33:8–9, 13, 18. To give just one of these instances, in Ezek. 3:18: "that wicked one will die for his sin" (*ho anomos ekeinos tēi adikiāi autou apothaneitai*).

a further judgment upon Achan's sin. Achan, therefore, is said in Joshua here not to have been the only one to die for his sin (Josh. 22:20). However, Jeremiah looks forward to a time when collective responsibility will give way to more individual responsibility, and "each person will die (only) for his own sin" (Jer. 31:30 [LXX 38:30]: *hekastos en tēi heautou hamartiāi apothaneitai*). This is already in place to a degree in the Torah. Deuteronomy expressly forbids vicarious death in this legal sphere: "Fathers shall not die for their children, and sons shall not die for their fathers; each person shall die for his own sin" (Deut. 24:16).[30] In this sense, Christ's death is *not* according to the Scriptures.

These passages, however, do lend weight to the view that *the language that Paul uses* should be understood as referring to vicarious death. There is a great variety of ways of expressing death as a result of sins (using, for example, the prepositions *dia*, *en*, or *huper*, or a simple dative without a preposition). Paul's language in Romans 4:25 taps into the pattern of references to death + *dia* + sins (cf. the case of Zelophehad above, as well as Isa. 53). In 1 Corinthians 15:3, Paul taps into another pattern, specifically that with the preposition *huper*, as where Zimri *died for the sins* that he had committed. The language in the case of Zimri is especially close to that of 1 Corinthians:

[Zimri] *apethanen huper tōn hamartiōn autou hōn epoiēsen.* (1 Kings 16:18–19 LXX)

[Christ] *apethanen huper tōn hamartiōn hēmōn.* (1 Cor. 15:3)

This language of "dying *huper*" is not exclusively biblical, as can be illustrated from an example cited by Versnel.[31] Paul's language

30. Here "for [*huper*] their children/fathers" might mean "in place of their children/fathers" in a purely substitutionary sense or "for what their children/fathers had done" in a broader sense. Philo (*Spec. Leg.* 3.153–54) sees both possibilities, with 2 Chron. 25:4 exploiting the broader meaning.

31. Lysias, *Against Eratosthenes* 78.4–5 (ca. 403 BCE): "Theramenes died not for [*huper*] you, but *as a result of his wickedness* [*huper tēs hautou ponērias*]." Clearly

in 1 Corinthians echoes the Old Testament language of dying in consequence of sins, even if Christ's death turns out to be a mirror image of the experience of Zimri and others like him.

3.3. Substitution in 1 Corinthians 15:3

Thus far we have seen the standard model, the norm according to which a person dies for his or her own sin(s). Alongside that, however, is the "aberration" that departs from the rule, namely, that of the suffering servant who dies for the sins of others. This aberration is picked up in Paul. There are two stages in the logic here: (1) Jesus died *because of* the sins of others, and (2) because he has done that, he thereby saves others from the consequence of sin.

Returning to Isaiah 53 and its connection with Paul, we have already begun to note that 1 Corinthians 15:3 is so similar to Isaiah 53 in various ways that it is easy to see a continuity of ideas. Like the servant, Christ died for the sins of others. The point in 1 Corinthians 15:3 is not that the death of Jesus was historically or legally caused by the sins of others in the sense that they killed him through their persecution. Paul includes the Corinthians in the "our" here, and so any sense in which the formula may have contained, in a Jewish-Christian context, an acknowledgment of legal responsibility for the death of Jesus is now absent.[32] Jesus's death is for Paul a *theological* consequence of sins rather than a straightforwardly historical one. By "theological" here I mean something that cannot be explained merely in terms of historical causation, for instance, Jesus dying as the result of the judicial verdicts of Herod, Pilate, and others. It is caused by others in another sense, however. Christ's death for

---

the first *huper* means "for the sake of" and the second "as a result of" (Versnel, "Making Sense of Jesus' Death," 230n67). The phrase *huper hamartiōn* is also causal in Pr. Man. 7.

32. Peter talked to the Jews on the day of Pentecost of "this Jesus whom you crucified" (Acts 2:36). It would be difficult for Paul to talk this way to the Corinthians unless he meant it in a different sense.

sins is theological because the divinely ordained consequence of sins is always death. Compare again Zimri, who "died for the sins which he had committed," and Zelophehad, who "died for his own sin."[33] Christ bore sins and died as a consequence. Through that, he thereby *deals with* sins—that is the purpose of his death. Just as the servant died in consequence of sins—bearing them in line with divine providence—so did Jesus, although there is no emphasis in Paul on the historical cause because of the universal scope of the sins. Similarly, just as the servant's death brought peace and healing through his bearing of iniquities, so Jesus's death dealt with others' sins through the very death that was the consequence of them.

Clearly the sins in question are not Christ's own but those of others. As a result, his death is clearly one that comes through his standing in the place of others. This comes out again in the alternation of the third-person singular with the first-person plural: "*he* died for *our* sins." The default Old Testament position would be "*he* died for *his* sins" or "*we* died for *our* sins." The miracle of the gospel, however, is that *he* died for *our* sins.

In sum, the death that is the theological consequence of sins came to him in our place. And it is precisely in his death in consequence of our sins that he takes them in our place and thereby deals with them. "For sins," then, means both *as a result of* sins and—therefore also—*to deal with* those sins. Because he has borne sins, we will not; because he has carried our sins and their theological consequence, we will not.

3.4. The Meaning of Christ Dying "Huper" Sins

One of the main reasons scholars have doubted the presence of substitution in Paul's letters is that the meaning of the preposition *huper* has (quite rightly) been said not necessarily to have

---

33. It might be noted that since death is the divine penalty for sins, the substitution here seems most likely to be *penal substitution*. As stated in the introduction, however, this point is not the contention in this volume.

substitutionary connotations in itself.[34] We will return in the next chapter to examine the meaning of *huper* in phrases that refer to Christ dying for *people*; here in this chapter we are concerned with the phrase "for *sins*."

We have seen above that the closest linguistic analogy for Paul's language in 1 Corinthians 15 is that language used of Zimri's death. We can see the two statements in parallel again:

> Zimri died for his sins, which he had committed.
> [Zimri] *apethanen huper tōn hamartiōn autou hōn epoiēsen.* (1 Kings 16:18–19 LXX)

> Christ died for our sins.
> [Christ] *apethanen huper tōn hamartiōn hēmōn.* (1 Cor. 15:3)

It is clear here that *huper* does not *in itself* have a substitutionary sense. The comparison in this chapter is between dying-*huper*-sins in the Old Testament and the same language in 1 Corinthians; both instances of the phrase mean "dying *in consequence of* sins." It is when this is set in the framework of *one person* doing this for the sins *of others* (*and not for one's own*) that the substitutionary sense is achieved. Moreover, when it is *Christ* who dies for our sins, the sense is not only that Christ died *in consequence of* our sins but that because of this he also thereby deals with them once and for all. Since "Christ died for our sins," it is no longer the case that we will die for them.[35]

34. Bieringer, "Traditionsgeschichtlicher Ursprung," 232; G. Röhser, *Stellvertretung im Neuen Testament* (Stuttgart: Verlag Katholisches Bibelwerk, 2002), 91. C. Breytenbach, "Versöhnung, Stellvertretung und Sühne: Semantische und traditionsgeschichtliche Bemerkungen am Beispiel der paulinischen Briefe," *NTS* 39 (1993): 68, helpfully gives three meanings that might make sense in different Pauline contexts: (1) "for the preservation of"; (2) "to deal with," i.e., to take away (with reference to sins); (3) "in the place of," in a substitutionary sense.

35. There is a linguistic distinction between taking *huper* in the senses of (a) "as a result of" (i.e., taking the "sins" loosely as the *efficient* cause) and (b) "for the sake of" (i.e., dealing with "sins," as the final cause). Breytenbach, "Versöhnung, Stellvertretung und Sühne," 68, for example, states that 1 Cor. 15:3 should be taken in the latter, not the former, sense ("for our sins and not because of our sins"); also

3.5. Gese and Hofius on 1 Corinthians 15:3

1 Corinthians 15:3 is a good test for whether the Tübingen view works. It is here that we can see that the theory runs into problems. The Old Testament scholar Hartmut Gese, discussed in the previous chapter, provides an interpretation of 1 Corinthians 15:3 in the majestic conclusion to his atonement article.

> "Christ died for our sins in accordance with the scriptures" (1 Cor. 15:3b). Atonement is the sacrifice of life for the sake of making life whole. It brings the abyss of human life into union with the highest divine *doxa*. Human life that has [been] given over to death is consecrated by God's glory, and God's *doxa* shines forth in our mortal existence. Atonement means a corporate life—it is always the whole that is atoned for—and so it is not only that the individual comes to partake of the holy through God's atonement; the atoning death of Jesus is sufficient for us all, it has reconciled the world with God.[36]

This is marvelous stuff, but is it what 1 Corinthians 15:3 is all about? Here, Gese brushes aside human *sins* in favor of an apparently "deeper" concept of sin. However, 1 Corinthians 15:3–4 is precisely concerned with human sins, and this is not a one-off. As we saw in the previous chapter, the similar formulas in Romans 4:25, Galatians 1:4, and elsewhere use the same language: "he was delivered over *for our transgressions*," "he gave himself *for our sins*," and so on.

A different proposition appears in Hofius. In his most recent discussion of atonement and reconciliation, there is again a very clear contrast of Hofius's position over against the substitutionary view. He first describes a hypothetical interpretation of the "Christ died for our sins" formula in 1 Corinthians 15.

Breytenbach, "'Christus starb für uns': Zur Tradition und paulinischen Rezeption der sogenannten 'sterbeformeln,'" *NTS* 49 (2003): 447–75 (469). However, it is because the sins have the consequence that they do (viz., the death of Jesus) that they also are dealt with.

36. H. Gese, "The Atonement," in *Essays on Biblical Theology* (Minneapolis: Augsburg, 1981), 115.

Just as the Hebrew expression in Isaiah 53 [i.e., "bearing sin"] is used to describe the *substitutionary* "bearing" of *alien* guilt, so also in 1 Corinthians 15:3b—read in the light of Isaiah 53!—there is the language of *substitutionary* death for the sake of *alien* sin. Thus understood, the first line of the summary describes Christ's death as the penal consequence of "our" sins, and "our" sins as the reason and cause of his dying. Christ's death would thereby be interpreted as an instance of substitutionarily taking over guilt and punishment. Christ has taken the place of the guilty, who are liable to death because of their sin, and by surrendering his own life to death, he has freed them from the "burden" and thereby from the fatal consequences of their sin.[37]

So here is a fairly conventional account, in which the formula adopts the substitutionary meaning of Isaiah 53, and Paul adopts the substitutionary meaning of the formula. Hofius, however, thinks that it is completely wrong to see Paul as adopting this substitutionary sense. Hofius concedes that this may have been the meaning of the pre-Pauline formula handed on to Paul. In Paul's hands, however, it cannot mean this: "Paul himself, by contrast, certainly did *not* have this understanding. Paul rather wanted the statement of 1 Corinthians 15:3b to be understood in terms of his conception of 'inclusive place-taking.'"[38] In other words, recalling the discussion in chapter 1 above, Christ identifies himself with us in his death rather than excluding us from death. The same applies to the reference to "Christ gave himself for our sins" in Galatians 1:4,[39] and to Christ being "handed over for our trespasses" (Rom. 4:25).[40]

It is strange, however, that the meaning of this Isaianic language is required to undergo a significant change in meaning in order to fit with Paul's theology. Language expressing substitution becomes language expressing inclusive place-taking—but that language

37. Hofius, "Fourth Servant Song," 179.
38. Ibid.
39. Ibid., 179n65.
40. Ibid., 181–82.

itself remains the same. The original substitutionary sense of Isaiah 53 must be transformed by Paul into a "representative" or "inclusive" conception because Paul just cannot have shared the original substitutionary understanding of Isaiah 53. It is of course perfectly possible to hypothesize that a word or phrase can have different meanings in different contexts. However, we are not dealing with different contexts but a very similar phenomenon—a death for others. Here is a case of one totalizing interpretation of the shape of Pauline soteriology determining what individual passages are permitted to say.

So the relevance of the Tübingen model of atonement to 1 Corinthians 15 seems rather limited. Resurfacing here are some of the same problems that we saw in the apocalyptic interpretations of Galatians, where Christ giving himself "for our sins" (Gal. 1:4) was also taken to be relativized in preference for a different account of the plight and solution. It is more natural to see, as does Kertelge, continuity between the meanings of the pre-Pauline and Pauline formulations.[41]

4. Conclusion

We saw already in chapter 1 that reports of Paul's lack of interest in "sins" are greatly exaggerated. 1 Corinthians 15:3 raises a further problem for the view that for Paul the real plight is not really sins, because he defines the plight this way in a passage where he is explicitly stating what he views the gospel to be. We can now return to Paul's summary of the gospel in 1 Corinthians 15 with fresh eyes.

> Now, brothers and sisters, I want to remind you of the gospel I preached to you, which you received and on which you have taken your stand. By this gospel you are saved, if you hold firmly to the word I preached to you. Otherwise, you have believed in vain.

41. K. Kertelge, "Das Verständnis des Todes Jesu bei Paulus," in *Der Tod Jesu: Deutungen im Neuen Testament*, ed. J. Beutler (Freiburg: Herder, 1976), 118.

> For what I received I passed on to you as of first importance:
> that Christ died for our sins according to the Scriptures, that he
> was buried, that he was raised on the third day according to the
> Scriptures. . . .
> Whether, then, it was I or they, this is what we preach, and this
> is what you believed.

We have not talked in this chapter about the totality of the gospel
as Paul understands it in 1 Corinthians 15:3–4. We have not—as
Paul would have done—spelled out who this "Christ" is who is
the subject of the sentence. Nor have we gone into any detail at
all about the resurrection. For the purposes of this chapter, the
focus has been on the substitutionary death of Christ. But it is
still noteworthy that Paul assigns this vicarious death such high
importance.

There is considerable debate in scholarly circles about whether
there is a "center" to Paul's thought. Among those who think
there is one, there is debate about what that center is. A number
of options are given, such as justification and the righteousness of
God (Käsemann),[42] reconciliation (R. P. Martin),[43] or God acting
in Christ (Schreiner).[44] We may not have a "center" here in 1 Corinthians 15, but we do clearly have a statement that the gospel,
consisting of Christ's substitutionary death and his resurrection,
is *primary in Paul's proclamation*. This is what Paul means by
saying that he passed it on to the Corinthians "first" or "as of
first importance" in verse 3. It may be difficult to discover which
concept occupied the center of a dead person's brain, but Paul
himself tells us that the gospel as summarized in 1 Corinthians
15:3–4 (or 3–5) does have *primacy in his preaching*.

42. E. Käsemann, *New Testament Questions of Today* (London: SCM, 1979), 168–69.
43. R. P. Martin, "Center of Paul's Theology," in *Dictionary of Paul and His
Letters*, ed. G. Hawthorne, R. P. Martin, and D. Reid (Leicester: Inter-Varsity, 1993),
92–95, with a discussion of the issue. See also J. Plevnik, "The Center of Paul's
Theology," *CBQ* 51 (1989): 460–78, for discussion.
44. T. R. Schreiner, *Apostle of God's Glory in Christ* (Leicester: Inter-Varsity,
2001).

The substitutionary character of the death of Christ is evident from the fact that we have the statement "X dies *huper* the sins of Y." It is not that *huper* in itself has a substitutionary sense; this would in any sense be meaningless, as Christ is not dying in the place of the actual sins but in place of the people who are saved. The substitutionary meaning arises out of the unusual language of one person dying for the sins of others. It is perfectly natural in the Old Testament that a person die for his or her own sins, that is, in consequence of them, either as a judgment inflicted through the terrible majesty of the judicial procedure of law or by divine action sudden or providential. What is extraordinary is that a person dies for *another's* sins, especially given that it is forbidden by the Torah. In the premonitions of Isaiah 53, however, there is precedent for the miraculous salvation of others taking place through God's bringing the consequences of the sins of others onto an innocent individual. In this way, Christ dies both in consequence of the transgressions of others and in order to deal with those infractions of the divine will.

Excursus

An Objection—Why, Then, Do Christians Still Die?

There is an objection that might naturally arise here or in any discussion of substitution in general: How can it be claimed that Christ died in place of (or instead of) believers, if those believers still go on subsequently to die?[1] This might appear to be a powerful *prima facie* obstacle to accepting substitution.

The short answer is this: Paul does not simply think that believers go on subsequently to die! This is a point that of course requires some elaboration. Principally, there is an asymmetry or disparity between the kind of death that Christ died on the cross and the deaths that Christian believers die at the end of their lives. There are four elements that need to be seen in the background here: first, the way in which Paul describes the literal deaths of

1. Such an objection is expressed in M. D. Hooker, *Not Ashamed of the Gospel: New Testament Interpretations of the Death of Christ* (Carlisle: Paternoster, 1994), 28, and underlies the remarks in D. Brondos, *Paul on the Cross: Reconstructing the Apostle's Story of Redemption* (Minneapolis: Fortress, 2006), 108–9.

believers; second, the metaphorical deaths of believers; third, the way in which Paul describes the deaths of others; fourth, the way in which Paul describes the death of Christ.

First, when Paul writes of the deaths of believers, he very often uses a paraphrastic "euphemism" of sorts, which effectively undermines the fact of death. As is well known, he can talk of believers dying as merely "falling asleep"; this idiom appears five times in 1 Corinthians (11:30; 15:6, 18, 20, 51) and four times in 1 Thessalonians (4:13, 14, 15; 5:10), and a further development of the metaphor appears in Ephesians 5:14. (Compare the "sleeps" of Jairus's daughter and Lazarus.)[2] Another expression that functions in a similar way appears in Philippians: Paul imagines the possibility of dying ("death," "to die," in Phil. 1:20–21) but glosses this as "to depart and be with Christ" (1:23). It is not a "rule" that Paul never speaks in a literal manner of the deaths of believers, but he very often speaks in other language that relativizes the event of physical death.[3]

Second, there is the way in which Paul describes the metaphorical deaths of believers. Here the point is not so much about Paul's statements of "dying every day" in the course of his ministry (e.g., 2 Cor. 4:11–12)—such instances are perhaps part metaphor, part hyperbole. Rather the metaphorical usage refers to the death to sin and burial in baptism that occurs in Christian initiation (see esp. Rom. 6).

Third, Paul writes in Romans that "if you live according to the flesh, you will die" (Rom. 8:13). This is obviously a death different from the mere "passing" of believers. It would miss the point to

2. Mark 5:39/Matt. 9:24/Luke 8:52 (Jairus's daughter), and John 11:11–13 (Lazarus).

3. Human death has, of course, a finality as far as social relations in this world are concerned. In that sense it is natural that when Paul is discussing a practical rule in 1 Cor. 7:39, he simply speaks of the death of a husband leaving the wife to remarry; to refer to "sleep" in this context would undermine the point about the finality of death within the sphere of human relations. Similarly, in other places Paul refers to people dying to make a binary parallel to "living" or "being made alive" (e.g., Rom. 14:8; 1 Cor. 15:22, 36).

say in response to Romans 8:13, "Yes, of course that's true, Paul—everybody dies." Paul does not mean "die" in the everyday sense; he means something like "suffer the divinely ordained penalty for sin." As he puts it earlier in Romans, "the wages of sin is death" (Rom. 6:23; cf. 6:21; also 1:32).[4] Paul can contrast the destiny of believers as "life" with that of unbelievers as "death" (2 Cor. 2:16; cf. Rom. 8:6). It is the kind of death for which he elsewhere uses the verb *apollumi*, usually translated in English versions as "perish" (e.g., 1 Cor. 1:18; 2 Cor. 2:15; 4:3; cf. Phil. 3:19).

Fourth, it is noticeable that Jesus's death is never described in these terms of mere sleeping. This may be simply the happenstance of Paul's vocabulary, but Paul more probably thought that such usage would dilute the depth of Christ's death. (On the other hand, he does not refer to Jesus as "perishing" either, presumably because that verb—at the other end of the spectrum from "sleeping"—would be *too* final.) Referring to Christ's death, Paul simply uses the word *apothnēiskō*, one of the most common Greek words for "die."[5]

With these four categories in the background, we can draw some conclusions in response to the objection at hand: How can it be claimed that Christ died instead of believers, if those believers still go on subsequently to die? The main point to conclude is that believers *do* still go on to die death #1 above but will not "perish" (#3 above). The substitutionary death of Christ saves from death #3, but believers—at least those who do die—will still "fall asleep" and "depart to be with Christ"; for Paul, this of course is only true of those who do die before the parousia, whereas those who remain alive will simply be taken up rather like Enoch (1 Thess.

---

4. The point is valid here whether one takes the verse to refer to "the wages that one receives *as a penalty for sinning*" or to "the wages that Sin (as leader and paymaster) pays."

5. Other language is sometimes employed. For example, in focusing on the passivity of Jesus, Paul states that Christ is "handed over" (Rom. 4:25), or that, focusing on Jesus's active role in his death, "he gave himself" (Gal. 1:4; 2:20). This language neither intensifies nor mitigates the weight of the death (as the language of "perishing" and "falling asleep" do, respectively); the focus is on agency.

4:13–18; cf. Heb. 11:5). Both kinds of believers have of course been saved, for Paul, from "perishing." Christ has undergone a death like death #3 to save us from death #3; therefore death #1 is not nearly so serious—it is a mere falling asleep.

In addition to being like death #3, Christ's death is also like our death #2. Paul clearly says as much when he states that it is our *death to sin in baptism* that is the death "like his death" (Rom. 6:5). Although representative death is not the focus in this present book, it is important here to note that following Christ's death there is a crucial sense in which we do participate in that death, but our death is "only" a metaphorical one.[6]

The death of Christ, then, is comparable not to death #1 but to deaths #2 and #3. Christ's substitutionary death addresses the plight not of death #1 (at least not directly) but of death #3. It is like "perishing" in that it is the divinely ordained consequence of sin, although because of his resurrection Christ's death does not have the finality that Paul associates with the term "perish," which—as just noted—is applied only to unbelievers. Paul's description of Christ's substitutionary death in 1 Corinthians 15:3 makes good sense on analogy with "perishing" (death #3): just as Zimri "died for his sins," so also Christ died for sins, though not his own. Christ *did* in his substitutionary death release us from the destiny of perishing, though—for those who die before the parousia—not from falling asleep and departing to be with Christ. The objection we are addressing implies that our passing (death #1) is strongly analogous to Christ's death, but this is not the case.

---

6. I do not intend by the word "only" to imply that the content of the metaphorical death is unimportant—merely that it is not a literal death.

3

The Vicarious Death of Christ and Classical Parallels (Rom. 5:6–8)

We have seen thus far some critique (in chap. 1) of antisubstitutionary or nonsubstitutionary accounts of the atonement and a more positive statement arguing for substitution in chapter 2. There it was seen that Christ's death *for our sins*—in the sense of dying in consequence of our sins and not his own—was expressive of a substitutionary death in 1 Corinthians 15. The present chapter will argue for a similar conclusion on quite different grounds. Specifically, we will see that Paul elsewhere compares Jesus's death with other examples of noble deaths in classical literature. What we will observe is that Paul's language about Jesus dying "for us" echoes very closely the language used frequently in non-Christian literature to describe substitutionary or vicarious deaths. The starting point for the discussion of the present chapter is a section of Romans 5:

> For although we were still weak, yet at the right time, Christ died for the ungodly [*huper asebōn*]. For scarcely will anyone die for a

righteous person [*huper dikaiou*], though for a good person [*huper tou agathou*] someone might perhaps even dare [*tolmāi*] to die. But God demonstrates his love for us in that while we were yet sinners, Christ died for us [*huper hēmōn*]. (Rom. 5:6–8)

We can see from the reference to Christ's death in this passage a slight difference in the way salvation is expressed by comparison with 1 Corinthians 15:3. There, as we saw in the previous chapter, the expression used was "Christ died for *our sins*." Here in Romans 5, the language is actually of Christ dying not for sins but for people: verse 6, Christ died for the ungodly; verse 7, dying for a righteous person or for a good person; verse 8, Christ died for us. This means that we have to read these passages as communicating something subtly different. As noted at the beginning of chapter 2, the two explanations of Christ's death are not simply the same.[1] The main difference is that here Paul links the death of Christ with other heroic deaths from his cultural environment—what he refers to as the rare examples of deaths for good or righteous individuals.

The aim of this chapter is to explore the significance of this parallel that Paul draws between the death of Christ and these other vicarious deaths from the Greco-Roman world. This will further confirm the substitutionary character of Paul's understanding of the atonement. The previous chapter focused primarily on the Old Testament background to the death of Jesus and on how Paul used the language of the suffering servant to identify Jesus as a substitute for us. This chapter aims to show what Paul's explanation of the death of Christ has in common with portrayals of vicarious deaths in classical tradition and where it departs from that tradition. We will see that Jesus's death is both similar and different: it is comprehensible to a gentile as a substitutionary death like other, more familiar cases, but it is also a shocking instance of it. The

---

1. C. Eschner, *Gestorben und hingegeben „für" die Sünder: Die griechische Konzeption des Unheil abwendenden Sterbens und deren paulinische Aufnahme für die Deutung des Todes Jesu Christi* (Neukirchen-Vluyn: Neukirchener Verlag, 2010), 357.

reason for this chapter is that Paul in Romans 5:7–8 compares the death of Jesus with other possible heroic deaths that his Roman readers/hearers might have known of: rare cases in which heroes might sacrifice themselves for good or just people.[2]

Before proceeding to the substance of the exegesis that will argue for a substitutionary understanding of the deaths in these verses, we need to address a translational matter.

1. The Translation of Romans 5:6–8

The preliminary question of translation to be cleared up is specifically of Romans 5:7.[3] English translations here, following the Authorized Version, talk of the extreme unlikelihood of death for a righteous person while leaving open the slightly more likely possibility of death on behalf of a good person.

> For scarcely for a righteous man will one die: yet peradventure for a good man some would even dare to die. (KJV)

> Indeed, rarely will anyone die for a righteous person—though perhaps for a good person someone might actually dare to die. (NRSV)

> Very rarely will anyone die for a righteous person, though for a good person someone might possibly dare to die. (NIV)

> For one will scarcely die for a righteous person—though perhaps for a good person one would dare even to die. (ESV)

2. See C. Breytenbach, "The 'For Us' Phrases in Pauline Soteriology: Considering Their Background and Use," in J. van der Watt, ed., *Salvation in the New Testament: Perspectives on Soteriology* (Leiden: Brill, 2005), 178, for the point that Rom. 5:7 shows that Paul has knowledge of the Greek tradition of vicarious death.

3. On this matter, see in addition to the commentaries esp. F. Wisse, "The Righteous Man and the Good Man in Romans V.7," *NTS* 19 (1972–73): 91–93; Y. Landau, "Martyrdom in Paul's Religious Ethics: An Exegetical Commentary on Romans 5:7," *Immanuel: Ecumenical Theological Research Fraternity (Jerusalem)* 15 (1982–83): 24–38; A. D. Clarke, "The Good and the Just in Romans 5:7," *TynBul* 41 (1990): 128–42; C. P. Hammond Bammel, "Patristic Exegesis of Romans 5:7," *JTS* 47 (1996): 532–42; T. W. Martin, "The Good as God (Romans 5:7)," *JSNT* 25 (2002): 55–70.

There is seeming unanimity here; I have not been able to find an exception among English translations.[4] It is also probably the majority interpretation among the commentators.[5] Some have suggested an alternative to the second clause, however. To adapt the NIV:

> Very rarely will anyone die for a righteous person, though *for the sake of the good* someone might possibly dare to die.

There are various contentious issues in the interpretation, but the main one is the translational question. The present chapter seeks to elucidate the contrast between Christ's death and other vicarious deaths for others (rather than noble deaths for *causes*).[6] Therefore the key point here is whether "the good" is a person ("the good person") or a thing ("the good," "goodness," "what is good," "a good cause"). The issue is a grammatical one, that is, whether the Greek *tou agathou* should be understood as masculine (in which case a person is in view) or neuter (in which case "the good" is impersonal).[7] One might compare the very similar

4. In addition to those cited above, I have checked Tyndale's New Testament, the Geneva Bible, the RSV, NJB, NASB, and the Holman Christian Standard. The Bishops' Bible reflects the ambiguity of the Greek ("the righteous," "the good"); the same was true of the Vulgate. I have not even seen a footnote citing the alternative possibility.

5. Clarke, "Good and the Just," 128.

6. Clarke categorizes six interpretive options: (1) the good man is also the righteous man; (2) the good man is a more attractive object of sacrificial devotion than the righteous man; (3) as in (1), they are synonymous, but Paul qualifies his extreme statement in the first half of the verse; (4) the good is the good cause, not a person; (5) the good man is specifically one's benefactor; (6) the text is corrupt. See ibid., 128–33. To this one might add some of the patristic options noted in Bammel, e.g., (7) that the good (one) is Christ—the view of Rufinus, or (8) the Marcionite (?) view that the good is Christ in contrast to the "just" god of the Law, a view opposed by Jerome (Bammel, "Patristic Exegesis," 534, 535). Martin, "Good as God," adds (9) that "the Good one" is God, as the title of the article suggests.

7. Breytenbach states as beyond dispute the view that "the good" is neuter. See C. Breytenbach, "Versöhnung, Stellvertretung und Sühne: Semantische und traditionsgeschichtliche Bemerkungen am Beispiel der paulinischen Briefe," *NTS* 39 (1993): 68. The point is argued extensively by Eschner, *Gestorben und hingegeben*, 278–89, who presents a strong case that the death for "the good" is not contrasted with Jesus's death but that Christ's death *is* death for the good. She also makes the point that elsewhere in Paul *agathos* is not used of persons. Her argument merits close inspection.

dilemma in translating the Lord's prayer: Does one pray for deliverance "from the evil one" (taking *tou ponērou* as masculine) or "from evil" (taking it as neuter)?

In favor of taking the reference in Romans 5 as to a person ("the good man") are the following points:

1. The preceding "righteous one" is clearly a person, and so a corresponding "good one" is a natural parallel.
2. Romans 5:7 stands in parallel to the preceding reference to Christ dying for the ungodly in 5:6, which suggests personal references in 5:7.[8]
3. Similarly, the following verse 8 refers to Christ dying for us sinners, and so again it is people who are the objects of self-sacrificial love, suggesting that the same is in view in 5:7.[9]
4. The definite article in "*the* good person" can be accounted for as specifying death on behalf of a particular *type* rather than necessarily seeing a specific individual in view.[10]

In light of these points, then, it is best to side with the majority view and see Paul contrasting Christ's death with "pagan" views of dying on behalf of a righteous person or a good person—or, better, "the good person."

2. A Sketch of the Exegesis

In Romans 5:6–8 Paul compares and contrasts the death of Christ with dying for a righteous or good person. It is important to spell out what is involved in the comparison in verse 7 and what is not.

1. The contrast lies not in comparing Jesus's death with a classical tradition of death for one's country. Horace's words *dulce et*

8. Bammel, "Patristic Exegesis," 542n39.
9. Clarke, "Good and the Just," 130–31n7, noting the context of both verses 6 and 8.
10. C. F. D. Moule, *An Idiom Book of New Testament Greek* (Cambridge: Cambridge University Press, 1959), 111, is probably correct to see the article as deictic ("pointing out some familiar type or genus").

decorum est pro patria mori are now a catchphrase in English, but the idea of "dying for one's country" is not in view here in Paul. It is obvious from Romans 5:7 that it is death for another individual that is involved—dying for a (singular) righteous or good *person*.

2. Again, the fact that a person is involved in Paul's comparison means that Jesus's death is not likened to deaths for a particular *cause*, a noble ideal, whether of a Greek or Roman or Jewish sort. Romans 5:7 does not, then, correspond to Eleazar's injunction in 4 Maccabees that children of Abraham should die "for piety" (4 Macc. 6:22).

3. Nor is an *institution* in view in Romans 5:7 as an object worthy of protection, such as when, in 1 Maccabees, martyrs may die "for the covenant of our fathers" (1 Macc. 2:50). Again, Romans 5:7 is concerned with a more personal object of devotion.

4. Nor is a Jewish tradition of vicarious death a likely background. The Old Testament, as we have seen in chapter 2, does not have much to say about individuals dying for other individuals, and indeed in some contexts actually prohibits it.

5. Rather, in talking of one person dying for another good or righteous person, the most natural link in Romans 5 is with examples of vicarious death in classical texts (broadly understood). There are a number of such classical works, as we shall see, where this same substitutionary language is used. So it is very likely that Paul is tapping into a classical tradition here and comparing heroic vicarious deaths in the Greco-Roman world (real and literary) in verse 7 with the death of Jesus in verse 8.

So how do they compare? In what follows, we will see a set of examples of vicarious death in the Greco-Roman world and then make some comparisons with the death of Jesus.

3. Vicarious Deaths in Classical Tradition

There is space for only a small selection of instances of vicarious deaths here. For much of this material I am particularly indebted to an essay by Henk Versnel (probably about the same length as this book) that assembles a very helpful collection of examples and also has a sophisticated classification of the various shades of meaning in the various heroic deaths.[11] As was attempted in §2 above, he distinguishes "dying for a creed,"[12] which contrasts with "effective death," that is, dying for other *people*.[13] This subdivides into "patriotic death," that is, dying for other people where the people are one's nation, and "vicarious death," where the sense is more substitutionary. In the latter in particular, what makes the deaths substitutionary is that there are usually at work "divine or supernatural principles of compensation in that a life is *unconditionally required* in order to save that of another or others."[14] In §3.1 below we will see both literary and historical examples of this (at least as represented in the texts), and §§3.2–3 discuss theoretical treatments of the motif of substitutionary death by (mostly) philosophers.

3.1. Conjugal Love: Alcestis

The preeminent example of substitutionary death in classical literature is the character of Alcestis.[15] The main impulse for her popularity was the play, called the *Alcestis* after its heroine, written by Euripides in about 438 BCE. (This work has a special place in my heart because it was the first play I saw performed in Greek, at the impressionable age of thirteen.) In the opening speech of the play, the god Apollo announces that he has granted the main male character in the play, Admetus, the king of Pherae in northern Greece, the possibility of escaping imminent death

11. H. S. Versnel, "Making Sense of Jesus' Death: The Pagan Contribution," in J. Frey and J. Schröter, eds., *Deutungen des Todes Jesu im Neuen Testament* (Tübingen: Mohr, 2005), 215–94.

12. Ibid., 227–30 (§2:1).

13. Ibid., 230–53 (§2:2).

14. Ibid., 231–32.

15. For further comment on her, see ibid., 235–36, and the bibliography he provides in n. 84.

if he finds someone to take his place (11–14). Only Admetus's wife, Alcestis, was willing "to die for him" (*thanein pro keinou*, 18) even though, as she puts it, it was not necessary for her "to die for you" (*thanein huper sethen*, 284). Alcestis does this, though, in part because neither of Admetus's parents was willing to do it. At one point, Admetus rather uncharitably tears into his father for not dying for him. The father replies, "I have no obligation to die on your behalf" (*opheilō d' oukh huperthnēskein sethen*, 682). Admetus has not died for him, so his father does not owe a similar debt: "You have not died for this one [i.e., me]; so nor shall I for you" (*mē thnēisch' huper toud' andros, oud' egō pro sou*, 690). He even jokes that perhaps Admetus's plan is to go on marrying again and again in order to get wives to die in his place (*katthanein . . . huper sou*, 701–2). Throughout the play we have a number of references to the same language that we find in Paul— dying "on behalf of" (*huper*) another in the sense of "in place of" or "instead of." The play is full of this language of Alcestis dying instead of her husband, Admetus.

Is Admetus "Good"?

It might be thought that this is a vicarious death, but is Alcestis's death really "dying for a good or just man," as in Romans 5? The modern reader would more naturally assume that Alcestis is really dying for a scoundrel of a husband. Although it might be easy to mistake Admetus for a villain, in fact the characterization of Admetus is rather more complicated. We need to beware that we do not simply adopt the stance toward Admetus that his father does. Three heroic characteristics of Admetus in the play are drawn out in a 1998 article by M. Dyson in the *Journal of Hellenic Studies*.

The first is the extravagance of his grief. As Dyson puts it,

> This devotion [to Alcestis], not perhaps in itself very remarkable, he is prepared to take to truly extraordinary lengths: he will mourn for the rest of his life (336–7); reminders in art and dreams will keep her permanently present (348–56); he will eventually be buried by

her side in the very same coffin (363–8). . . . Euripides is making Admetus a paradigmatic instance of grief at its most extreme, and he gives him a character to suit, for he is rather more than a typical distracted husband. . . . Only a person who has something larger than life about him is capable of such a commitment [to remain chaste], and along with this he exhibits the intolerance often inseparable from the concentration necessary for high achievement. Again, his immoderate absorption in his grief is both strength and weakness at once.[16]

So this "immoderate absorption" reveals, in its classical dramatic context, his heroic temperament.

A second feature is his heroic hospitality. This is evident in Admetus's welcome of Heracles into his household even at the height of his grief. As Heracles says of Admetus,

> He welcomed me to his house, not sending me away,
> though afflicted with woeful circumstance;
> more—hiding it, noble in respect for me.
> Whose house is more generous in Thessaly,
> In all Greece? Nor shall this noble man
> Claim to be benefactor of an ingrate. (*Alc.* 855–60)

So Heracles praises Admetus's generosity, twice calling him "noble" (*gennaios*).

A final noble aspect of Admetus's character is his commitment to lifelong chastity. As she dies, Alcestis requests that Admetus not remarry so that the children do not have a stepmother inflicted upon them. A king like Admetus could still have concubines, and yet he promises not to. Here is Dyson again:

> First, Alcestis wants him to remain unmarried for the sake of the children (304–5). . . . His immediate response, however, leaps far beyond her request. His avowal that he wants no more children

---

16. M. Dyson, "Alcestis' Children and the Character of Admetus," *JHS* 108 (1988): 20, 21.

implies acceptance of her reasoning (334–5), and he accepts the role of mother-substitute (377–8), but his protestations of fidelity are based not on concern for the children but on his commitment to her as his wife: "I had you as my wife in life and you alone will be called my wife in death" (328–30). . . . It is this extravagant, passionate loyalty to her, excluding him not only from marriage but from any sexual relationship with women (1056–61), and even from their company (950–4), that he maintains throughout the play.[17]

Admetus goes well beyond the call of duty here. In addition to these three points raised by Dyson, one other might be noted. In the prologue, Apollo describes Admetus at the outset as a holy man (*hosiou . . . andros*) just as he, the god, is holy (*Alc.* 10). So a god calls him holy, and a demigod twice calls him noble. In sum, despite initial impressions, Admetus does fit rather well into Paul's language in Romans 5 about a heroic death for a good or righteous man—at least when such terms are understood within the framework of classical tragedy.

ALCESTIS IN PLATO

In addition to Euripides, the other most influential author to discuss Alcestis in antiquity was Plato, in the *Symposium* (about 384 BCE). This book is a highly entertaining account of a party in which each guest has to make a speech in praise of the god Eros. Phaedrus is the first to make a speech. He comments that if it could ever be possible to have a state or an army made up of lovers, then it would be unconquerable. Their bravery and nobility would be such that they would always be wanting to impress one another. It is only lovers—not only men but women as well—who would ever die for one another (*huperapothnēiskein*). So Plato, or Phaedrus at least, is perhaps similar to Paul in seeing vicarious death as a rarity.

Phaedrus gives as his proof the case of Alcestis. Not only is she a particularly good example in herself, but the play proves the

17. Ibid., 20.

point particularly well because of the contrast between Alcestis, who was willing to die for Admetus (*huper tou autēs andros apothanein*), and Admetus's parents, who were not (179b–c). Lovers might venture to die on behalf of each other, but parents will not, at least according to Phaedrus.

"Daring" to Die

A further connection with Paul's vocabulary in Romans 5 appears in the *Symposium*.[18] Plato goes on to contrast Alcestis favorably with Orpheus, who wanted to be reunited with his dead wife Eurydice. Orpheus, however, at least in Plato's version, was a coward in being unwilling to be reunited with her by dying and instead negotiating a visit to the underworld during his lifetime. As a result, he did not "dare" (*tolmān*) to die out of love for Eurydice as Alcestis did for Admetus. Moving on several centuries, Plutarch echoes Plato's language in his use of some of the same language about Alcestis, noting that she "dared" (*tolmān*) even to die for her husband.[19]

Alcestis in the First and Second Centuries CE

In addition to Plutarch's reference, there are various other indications that the memory of Alcestis was still popular in Pauline times.[20] In particular, a set of inscriptions from the first century CE in Sardinia (IG XIV 607) honors a woman called Pomptilla, who died to save her sick husband from death. One states, "Pomptilla died as a ransom for her sweet husband" (*thanein men Pōmptillan glukerou lutron huper gametou*). Another likens her to Alcestis. Similarly, in a second-century CE inscription from Odessa, a hus-

18. Landau is correct that "daring" here in Romans 5 is not "venturing" in a weak sense but a reference to "heroic courage" ("Martyrdom in Paul's Religious Ethics," 33), a point strengthened by the parallels noted above.

19. Plutarch, *Dialogue on Love* (*Mor.* 761E).

20. For these references, see especially the insightful discussions of H. S. Versnel, in "Self-Sacrifice, Compensation and the Anonymous Gods," in *Le sacrifice dans l'antiquité*, by J.-P. Vernant et al. (Geneva: Vandœvres, 1980), 165; Versnel, "Making Sense of Jesus' Death," 240–41, which lists the relevant statements in the inscriptions.

band has inscribed as part of the epitaph of his wife, "Now in my place she has died [*ant' emou thnēiskei*] and has fame and praise like Alcestis."[21] In a later example of uncertain date, there is a woman Callicratia, who like Pomptilla has apparently somehow died for her husband:

> I am a new Alcestis, and died for my good [*esthlou*]
>   husband
> Zeno, whom alone I had taken to my breast. My
> heart preferred him to the light of day and my sweet
> children. My name was Callicratia, and all men
> reverenced me.[22]

She is, therefore, imagined as talking about herself as "a new Alcestis" because she died in the place of her husband.

We have no idea what happened that made these substitutions possible; it is actually very rare in the natural sphere that someone might have the opportunity to die in place of another. One possibility is that these wives may have made vows to the gods to die if their husbands were granted recovery from a potentially fatal illness—vows that they might fulfill by "coincidence, suicide, disease, or autosuggestion."[23]

Alcestis is also discussed by philosophers in Paul's day. An exact contemporary of Paul, the philosopher Musonius Rufus, uses Alcestis as illustration of how excellent an estate marriage is.[24] Shortly after this, toward the end of the first or the early second century CE, comes the reference in Plutarch already mentioned.

In conclusion, then, perhaps the most well-established example of substitutionary death for pagans in Paul's day was that of

21. IGBulg I² 222, lines 11–14. For the dating, text, translation, and commentary, see W. M. Calder III, "The Alkestis Inscription from Odessos: IGBR I² 222," *AJA* 79 (1975): 80–83.

22. *Greek Anthology* 7.691.

23. Versnel, "Self-Sacrifice, Compensation and the Anonymous Gods," 165, and Versnel, "Making Sense of Jesus' Death," 241n105, citing W. M. Calder III.

24. Musonius Rufus 14.

Alcestis, who—like the rare case in Romans 5:7—"dared" sufficiently that she was willing "to die for a good man," just as Pomptilla apparently died for her "sweet husband" and Callicratia for
her "good husband." As has been known in scholarship for some
time, Alcestis was not merely an obscure literary character but
was "part of common culture."[25] She may even be the particular
case Paul has in mind.

3.2. Friendship

Paul and Plato, then, are in some agreement that vicarious death
is something of a rarity. Paul imagines someone might be willing
to die for a good or righteous person; Plato's character Phaedrus
thinks that only lovers would consider it. Other philosophical
traditions maintain that vicarious deaths are more common than
Plato and Paul allow.

Diodorus Siculus, writing in the first century BCE, says that
Pythagoreans made a habit of doing whatever they could for their
fellows—even dying for each other. The story of Phintias and
Damon was widespread in Greek and Latin literature.[26] Phintias
was due the death penalty but offered the willing Damon as surety
for his death while he was putting his affairs in order.

> While Dionysius was tyrant [of Syracuse, in the fourth century],
> a certain Phintias, a Pythagorean, had plotted against the tyrant.
> When he was on the point of receiving his punishment, he asked
> Dionysius for time so that he could deal with his private affairs as
> he wished. He said that he would offer one of his friends as surety
> for his death. The ruler marvelled at the prospect of there being
> such a friend who would offer himself to the prison in his place.

25. C. Breytenbach, "The Septuagint Version of Isaiah 53 and the Early Christian
Formula 'He Was Delivered for Our Trespasses,'" *NovT* 51 (2009): 341. See already
the collection of material in Calder, "Alkestis Inscription," 81–82, and S. Wood, "Alcestis on Roman Sarcophagi," *AJA* 82 (1978): 499–510. On the reception of Euripides
more generally in the period, see Versnel, "Making Sense of Jesus' Death," 224n43.

26. E.g., Cicero, *Off.* 3.45; *Tusc. Disp.* 5.22 (cf. Iamblichus, *Pyth.* 233–36; Hy-
ginus, *Fab.* 257).

Phintias summoned one of his acquaintances—Damon by name,
a Pythagorean philosopher, who without hesitation came forward
at once as surety for his death.[27]

In some versions of the story, Dionysius is so impressed by this
that he lets Phintias off and wants to be friends with both of these
Pythagoreans. Dionysius clearly regarded this act as a marvelous
rarity.

In the passage above, Phintias and Damon are described not
only as philosophical colleagues but also as "friends." This theme
of friendship (*philia*) was one of the most important in Greek and
Roman philosophy at the time of the New Testament and before.
It is not exactly the same as modern friendship. (Still less does
it overlap with the debased coinage of Facebook "friendship"!)
Rather, in addition to a straightforward mutual affection, it often
also involved an array of mutual responsibilities and reciprocal
social requirements. Simon Goldhill describes the "friend" (*philos*)
as follows:

The appellation or categorization *philos* is used to mark not just
affection but overridingly a series of complex obligations, duties,
and claims.[28]

So, for example, one's fellow countrymen can be "friends." In
some cases, even if one has not met them before, they can still be
friends in a technical sense.

A prime example of this is the encounter between Glaucus and
Diomedes in the Trojan War in Homer's *Iliad*. These two warriors
come face-to-face for combat. Diomedes asks the identity of his
enemy, not having seen him before. He is slightly nervous that
this enemy might be a god, whom he would not wish to fight.

27. Diodorus Siculus 10.4 (writing ca. 60–30 BCE). I have modified the translation
in C. H. Oldfather, *Diodorus Siculus: Library of History, Volume IV, Books 9–12.40*,
LCL (Cambridge, MA: Harvard University Press, 1946).
28. S. D. Goldhill, *Reading Greek Tragedy* (Cambridge: Cambridge University
Press, 1986), 82.

Glaucus replies with quite a lot of information: there was once a man Aeolus, who begat Sisyphus, who begat (a different) Glaucus, who begat Bellerophon, who begat Hippolochus, who begat the Lycian general Glaucus now fighting for Troy. The key relation here is Bellerophon, Glaucus's grandfather. Unexpectedly, Diomedes—whose grandfather was Oeneus—responds with delight to Glaucus's account of his genealogy as follows:

> Well then, you are now a friend [*xeinos*] of my father's house of long standing: for noble Oeneus once entertained incomparable Bellerophon in his halls, and kept him twenty days; and moreover they gave one another fair gifts of friendship. Oeneus gave a belt bright with scarlet, and Bellerophon a two-handled cup of gold which I left in my palace as I came here. . . . Therefore now I am a dear guest-friend [*xeinos philos*] to you in the centre of Argos, and you to me in Lycia, whenever I come to the land of that people. So let us shun one another's spears even among the throng; for there are many for me to slay, both Trojans and famed allies, whomever a god shall grant me and my feet overtake; and as many Achaeans in turn for you to slay, whomever you can. And let us make exchange of armor with each other, so that these men too may know that we declare ourselves to be friends [*xeinoi*] from our fathers' days. (*Il.* 6.215–31)[29]

Diomedes and Glaucus, therefore, realize that even though they have never met before, they are in the technical sense "friends" or "guest-friends."[30] The alliance forged between Bellerophon and Oeneus, their grandfathers, established a bond overriding their immediate conflict.

One of the questions about friendship discussed by philosophers was whether friends ought to be willing to die for one another, and a number answered the question in the affirmative. According

---

29. Translation from Homer, *Iliad: Books 1–12*, trans. A. T. Murray, rev. W. F. Wyatt, LCL (Cambridge, MA: Harvard University Press, 1999).

30. The term *xe(i)nos* is closely related to *philos*. See Goldhill, *Reading Greek Tragedy*, 81–82.

to Diogenes Laertius, the Stoic disciples of Zeno believed that a person should be willing to die on his country's behalf or "for his friends" (*huper philōn*).[31] Toxaris, a character in Lucian's work on friendship, takes pride in the fact that his fellow Scythians provide many examples of "deaths for friends" (*thanatous huper tōn philōn*).[32]

Friendship tends to be individualistic in philosophical literature, where it is a major theme.[33] From the first century, around the time of Paul, one can mention Epictetus and Seneca. Epictetus writes as follows in a discussion of how divination ought (or rather, ought not) to be used:

> Through an unreasonable regard to divination many of us omit many duties. For what more can the diviner see than death or danger or disease, generally things of that kind? If then I must expose myself to danger for a friend, and if it is my duty even to die for him, what need have I then for divination?[34]

Notice the words "must" and "duty": Epictetus takes it for granted that a friend should be willing to face danger and even death for another friend.

Similarly, Seneca writes,

> For what purpose, then, do I make a man my friend? In order to have someone for whom I may die, whom I may follow into exile, against whose death I may stake my own life, and pay the pledge too.[35]

For Seneca, "to have someone for whom to die" is the very reason for friendship.

31. Diogenes Laertius, *V.P.* 7.130 (mid-third century CE).
32. Lucian, *Toxaris* 36 (ca. 163 CE).
33. M. Wolter, "Der Heilstod Jesu als theologisches Argument," in *Deutungen des Todes Jesu im Neuen Testament*, ed. J. Frey and J. Schröter (Tübingen: Mohr Siebeck, 2005), 302, notes that friendship ethics lies behind Rom. 5:7.
34. Epictetus, *Diss.* 2.7.3.
35. Seneca, *Epistle* 9.10.

One example I have not seen mentioned in Pauline discussions is attributed to Epicurus (341–270 BCE). Because of the avowed priority of pleasure and the absence of physical or mental pain as the goal of human life, it is perhaps hard to understand how exactly a notion of death for friends might fit in with Epicureanism. Nevertheless, in a list of the responsibilities of the wise man, Epicurus states that the sage should at any time die for a friend (*huper philou pote tethnēxesthai*).[36] One possibility might be that tranquility and absence of fear could reach a high point if one were convinced that a friend might die for you. Even if it is highly unlikely that the need or possibility of another dying in your place should ever arise, it would nevertheless be reassuring to know that someone in theory might. Although not discussing this saying about vicarious death, one scholar has written, "Epicurus himself draws attention to the intangible rewards (of friendship) when he emphasises that a feeling of confidence (*pistis*) about help in need to come is more important than the help itself."[37] In other words, it may be the feeling of confidence rather than the actual vicarious death itself that is the key thing in Epicureanism. Another possibility is that being dead is simply no bad thing if one is an Epicurean![38] This doctrinal problem relates to our next example as well, from another Epicurean.

3.3. Death for Family Members: Philonides

This Epicurean text is a fragment from among the carbonized Herculaneum papyri buried by the eruption of Mount Vesuvius in 79 CE. It is a life of the Epicurean philosopher Philonides, who flourished in the second century BCE. His biography was written not long after his death: the manuscript has been dated to the first

36. Diogenes Laertius, *V.P.* 10.121 = Usener, frag. 590 of Epicurus.
37. J. M. Rist, "Epicurus on Friendship," *Classical Philology* 75 (1980): 124.
38. I am grateful to Dr. James Warren in the Faculty of Classics in Cambridge for raising this possibility.

century BCE.[39] Philonides is probably the speaker here, talking about his brother:

> [For] the most beloved of one's kinsmen or friends, he would readily offer his neck. For if it were proper for me to die for my native-land, how could I not also die for a kinsman?[40]

The immediate reference here is probably to Philonides's love for his brother Dicaearchus, who is mentioned in the previous fragment and later in this present one.

3.4. Summary

In sum, we can see a consistency of language used to describe vicarious deaths, and we have a number of different examples. The earliest example we have looked at goes back to the glory days of classical Athens in the fifth century BCE, in Euripides's *Alcestis*. A great deal changes in the five hundred years between Euripides and Paul, but interestingly the tale of Alcestis endures, and she continues to be described as a heroine up to the time of Paul in the first century. We can see this in Musonius Rufus (an exact contemporary of Paul) and the Pomptilla inscriptions. The ideal of death for a friend is held across a wide spectrum of philosophical schools; we have seen examples from Pythagoreans, Stoics, and Epicureans, and the cases we have looked at include Stoics and Epicureans from around the time of Paul. As we noted, the surviving copy of the life of the Epicurean Philonides comes from the first century BCE, and the Stoics Seneca and Epictetus make comments about substitutionary death for friends in the first century CE. So the historical links between Paul and the classical

---

39. The copy dates "allo scorcio del primo sec. a.C." (end of the first century BCE). See I. Gallo, "Vita di Filonide Epicureo," in *Studi di papirologia ercolanese* (Naples: M. D'Autia Editore, 2002), 63, who makes the judgment about date on the basis of Cavallo.

40. The Greek here is *huper anagkaiou*. P. Hercul. 1044, frag. 22, lines 7–11. Text in Gallo, "Vita di Filonide Epicureo," 119.

authors we have discussed are close. We do not know if Paul actually knew any of these works or whether the idea of death in someone's place and some of the characters like Alcestis were just part of the atmosphere. In either case, such works and characters provide a fitting background to Paul's language in Romans 5.

4. The Comparison in Romans 5:6–8

We have, then, three main contexts for vicarious or substitutionary deaths in the Greco-Roman world: conjugal love; the institution of friendship, which includes both the more theoretical philosophical discussions and the Pythagoreans who were willing to die for one another; and family ties. (I realized only after finding these examples, and ordering them this way, that they correspond to three of C. S. Lewis's "four loves"—*erōs*, *philia*, and *storgē*.)[41] We can return to the question posed earlier. How do they compare with what Paul says about Jesus's death? Let us recall the passage, Romans 5:6–8:

> For although we were still weak, yet at the right time, Christ died for the ungodly. For scarcely will anyone die for a righteous person, though for a good person someone might perhaps even dare to die. But God demonstrates his love [*agapē*] for us in that while we were yet sinners, Christ died for us [*Christos huper hēmōn apethanen*].

So how do these classical writers compare with Paul? As we have already noted, in one sense *positively*. There is a clear point of similarity in the analogy that Paul makes in Romans 5. It is essential to any comparison that there are points of similarity and points of dissimilarity. Without dissimilarity a comparison is meaningless, but without similarity a comparison is simply impossible. It is difficult, perhaps impossible, to compare a hedgehog with Fermat's

---

41. C. S. Lewis, *The Four Loves* (London: Geoffrey Bles, 1960). My ordering was simply the order in which I encountered them.

Last Theorem, for example. Paul sees that there is common ground between these pagan instances and the death of Christ, otherwise the analogy simply would not work. The common ground is that there is a death of one person for others. The sacrificial death of the one aims at rescuing the other from death. The most obvious indication that Paul is talking about substitutionary deaths of Jesus and of other heroic figures in Romans 5 is that they employ the same language of X "dying for" Y. Paul also acknowledges the bravery involved in the heroic deaths of these pagans: "*for a good person* [*huper tou agathou*] someone might perhaps even *dare to die* [*tolmāi apothanein*]," and again that same terminology appears in the classical writers. Paul is apparently comparing one substitutionary death with other substitutionary deaths.

For Paul the differences are more striking than the similarities, however, and in Romans 5 he is obviously focusing on how radically different Jesus's death is from any heroic death in the classical tradition. We can begin with heroic deaths at the instigation of Eros. Alcestis and Admetus are a great example of marriage. The philosopher Musonius Rufus holds their marriage up as a model— the institution must be great if it can produce such a magnificent form of loving self-sacrifice. Plato includes Alcestis as an example of one who has clearly been inspired by the god Eros—without such divine inspiration, her act of self-sacrifice for her husband would not and could not happen. The Greek or Roman philosopher, however, would certainly be baffled by a death for an *enemy*. Yet this is the miraculous point to which Paul draws attention in Romans 5: "while we were *enemies*, we were reconciled to God through the death of his Son" (5:10).

Or we can consider death for a *friend*, as discussed by Paul's contemporaries Seneca and Epictetus. As noted above, friendship was based not only on affection but also on a complex set of social obligations—but here again the parallel with Jesus breaks down. Our failure in our obligation to worship God as he deserved had created a rupture in the *philia* relationship, the bond of friendship.

This is emphasized in another description of us in Romans 5:8: "God established his love for us in the fact that while we were *sinners*, Christ died for us." Picture the baffled Cicero or Seneca trying to make sense of this person called Jesus dying for people who had renounced all the obligations of the relationship—to such an extent that the relationship no longer existed in anything like its original form. They would struggle to understand how this Jesus could possibly die for people who had desecrated the name of his father (Rom. 1:22–23).[42] The same applies in the case of death for a kinsman, a requirement for Philonides, which also fails to correspond adequately to Paul's account of Christ's death in Romans 5.

Another adjective that is used of us in Romans 5 is "ungodly," "unholy," or "impious" (*asebēs*). Much the same applies here as with the others—again, it would be unthinkable to lay down one's life for the impious. These are the people who in a number of strands of Greek and Roman thought endanger the gods' approval of the nation; they bring pollution, *miasma*, upon the whole community. And in consequence of this pollution, they invite *nemesis* from the gods, divine vengeance, upon their city or nation. Far from being objects of love, they should be shunned and exiled. As Paul puts it, for a "good man" or a "righteous man," a pagan might possibly dare to die, but not for one who is impious.

4.1. Summary

In sum, it is not simply that Jesus's death differs from these heroic Greek and Roman deaths. Many of the same elements are there. The theme of vicarious death overall, however, is radically subverted by Paul. In the examples from classical literature, there

---

42. Of course Jesus says in John 15:13, "Greater love has no one than this, that he lay down his life for his friends." One difference between John and Paul here is that Jesus has earlier in John 15 stated that he has made his disciples clean through his word (15:3), perhaps in anticipation of—or as some kind of proleptic instance of—laying down his life for them.

is first the relationship, and this relationship provides the context that makes the vicarious death at least understandable, even if it is still heroic. In the case of the Christ, however, his death does not conform to any existing philosophical norm. In Romans 5, Christ's death creates a friendship where there had been enmity.

This is something like the point Paul makes further on in the passage, in Romans 5:9–10:

> Therefore, having been justified by his blood, how much more will we be saved from God's wrath through it. For if when we were enemies we were reconciled to God through the death of his Son, how much more having been reconciled, will we be saved by his life.

Now that Christ has died for us, we have a relationship with God in which this future hope is guaranteed. As the passage goes on, this hope is rooted in the relationship that we have with God—we now boast, or rejoice, or exult in him.

5. Conclusion

As noted in the beginning, Paul's language in Romans 5 requires a different background, a different point of comparison from that of 1 Corinthians 15 in the previous chapter. The reference to the death of Christ in Romans 5 does not evoke the suffering servant in Isaiah 53 but rather invites comparison with the examples of noble vicarious deaths from Paul's cultural environment. We have seen a number of cases of such substitutionary deaths, and Paul is concerned to emphasize how different in kind Jesus's self-giving death for the impious enemies of God is from the comparatively conventional (but still heroic) noble deaths in classical literature. Nevertheless, it is striking how in the terminology that they all use—Paul and classical authors alike—there is a lot of language shared in common. In the cases we have examined, the death "for" another is not merely a death "for the benefit of" another—"for their sake" in a general sense. Nor is it death *with* them. Rather, it is what Eschner has called a "doom-averting death," a death that averts death.[43] These examples, then, are all about one person who stands in the place of another, and so they offer a useful parallel to and background for Paul's substitutionary conception of Jesus's death. For Paul's comparison in Romans 5:6–8 to make sense, we must see Paul comparing the substitutionary deaths of others with the substitutionary death of Jesus.

43. Eschner, *Gestorben und hingegeben*, 347.

Conclusion

It merely remains to sum up the main conclusions of the forego-ing chapters. The introduction began by defining substitution as—in the present discussion—Jesus dying instead of sinners. It is therefore different from *representation*, according to which Jesus identifies with sinners such that when he dies, they in some sense die with him. (Although different from each other, there is, however, no reason why substitutionary and representative under-standings of the atonement might not happily coexist.) Among various objections that may be lodged against substitution, the most important one for the present discussion is the *exegetical* objection, that is, the claim that Jesus's substitutionary death is not a biblical idea. The present book has aimed briefly to address this claim and to show that in fact Paul's letters do attest such a death of Jesus in our stead.

Chapter 1 focused on three theories that in different ways are either nonsubstitutionary or antisubstitutionary. The first, what was labeled as the Tübingen view, presented Jesus's death as an act of identification with human beings in which Jesus goes through judgment on behalf of, though not instead of, others. In Jesus, others go through this judgment of death and out the other side in order to be reconciled with God. The second view, that of interchange, argued that Paul was opposed to a substitutionary understanding and instead viewed Jesus as identifying with human beings in their Adamic condition of sin and death, joining with them but also, through his resurrection, bringing them back into right relationship with God. Finally, the apocalyptic view of Pauline soteriology—at least in some formulations of it—argued that substitution does not address the present state of humanity as already under a curse, does not sufficiently account for the enslaved plight of humanity, or is too closely tied to a forensic understanding of Paul's thought. In addition to particular difficulties attending these individual views, all of them suffer to a greater or lesser extent from a common failing: they downplay or neglect how the cross deals not only with *Sin* but also with individual *sins*. It has been argued here that contrary to certain strands of New Testament scholarship, Paul viewed these transgressions as serious and in need of a radical solution.

Against the backdrop of these understandings of the death of Jesus, chapters 2 and 3 aimed to put substitution back into a proper understanding of Pauline soteriology. Through an exegesis of 1 Corinthians 15:3, chapter 2 set out to see Jesus's death as bearing the consequences of sins. Among the various forms of words that the Old Testament uses to describe human deaths for sins, the formula in 1 Corinthians taps into one particular case— dying *huper* ("for") sins. So in some respects, Christ dies for sins in the same way that sinful individuals in the Old Testament die for sins. However, Isaiah 53 leads to a significant modification of this Old Testament form of words: Christ is of course not dying for his own sins but rather—like the suffering servant—for the sins of others. Because he died in consequence of our sins, we will not. As a result, his death not only is the result of our sins but also thereby deals with them. He bore our sins in our stead so that we will not.

Chapter 3 dealt with Romans 5:6–8, which, in contrast to 1 Co-rinthians 15:3, was not to be understood against an Old Testament background. Rather, in the Romans passage, Paul compares and con-trasts the death of Jesus with vicarious deaths in the Greco-Roman world, specifically those cases in which one person dies heroically in the place of another, as in the case of Alcestis. In addition to the examples of vicarious deaths represented in literature and that come to be seen as such in history, philosophers in particular also reflect upon vicarious death as a virtuous act. Although Jesus's death is presented by Paul as quite different from these because it is a death for enemies, Jesus's death is at least comparable in that it is a death in the place of others. Paul and all these other authors use the same language, representing alike the deaths as substitutionary. Therefore, again, Jesus died so that we should not.

In sum, substitution can and should be regarded as integral to the biblical picture of the atonement. According to Romans 5:8, Jesus's substitutionary death is God's demonstration of his love toward us. In 1 Corinthians 15:1–4, it is part of Paul's summary of the gospel, the gospel that is "of first importance."

Finally, if Jesus's death is indeed understood as substitutionary in Paul's letters, we need to get away from an unhelpful either/or that forces us to choose between representation and substitu-tion or between "apocalyptic" liberation and substitution. This is not to say that it is a simple matter to weave the two together into a seamless garment. Some might argue that substitution is rooted in representation.[1] Or again, perhaps substitution, with its related concept of forgiveness, is a preparation for liberation, rather as Israel's suffering for her sins precedes rescue from exile in Isaiah 40 and forgiveness of sins leads to "times of refreshing" (Acts 3:18–20). The logic of Galatians 1:4 might suggest that Jesus's giving himself for our sins is preparatory to deliverance

---

1. E.g., N. T. Wright, *Paul and the Faithfulness of God* (London: SPCK, 2013), 865: "*Because* he is Israel's representative, he can be the appropriate substitute, can take on himself the curse of others, so they do not bear it any more." Emphasis original.

from the present evil age.[2] But while some scholars have seen the substitutionary and participatory dimensions of Paul's thought as amenable to integration, others have seen them as running in parallel without ever meeting or assume that Paul must have held only to one of the two.[3]

Even if the precise relations of substitution, representation, and liberation may be unclear, there is no reason all three cannot simultaneously inhabit Paul's thought and biblical theology more broadly. It is striking how, when Paul comes to summarize his gospel in 1 Corinthians 15, he describes how Christ's substitutionary death has dealt with sins (15:3) and in the same chapter also goes on to focus on the ultimate conquest of the "last enemy to be defeated," death (15:26). Similarly, as was noted earlier, Colossians 2:13–15 juxtaposes forgiveness of sins with Christ's stripping of the principalities and powers. In much the same way, the Heidelberg Catechism gives the following question and answer at its beginning, identifying the work of Jesus as both dealing with *sins* and effecting liberation from *Sin*.

Q: What is your only comfort in life and in death?

A: That I, with body and soul, both in life and in death, am not my own, but belong to my faithful Saviour Jesus Christ, *who with His precious blood has fully satisfied for all my sins, and redeemed me from all the power of the devil*.[4]

In closing, one need only note that the choice between salvation as dealing both with "trespasses" or "debts" (plural) and with

2. See further S. J. Gathercole, "Justification by Faith," in *The Oxford Handbook to Paul*, ed. R. B. Matlock (Oxford: Oxford University Press, forthcoming).

3. For an argument for the incommensurability of the two, see esp. D. A. Campbell, *The Deliverance of God* (Grand Rapids: Eerdmans, 2009). On the other hand, R. B. Matlock has commented on a related dichotomy: "The interrelation of 'justification' and 'participation' has often enough been affirmed in the exegetical literature, though without consensus." See Matlock, "Zeal for Paul but Not according to Knowledge: Douglas Campbell's War on 'Justification Theory,'" *JSNT* 34 (2011): 147n60.

4. Heidelberg Catechism, Question 1. The italics are, of course, my own.

liberation from the power of (the) evil (one) was a choice apparently not faced by Jesus in his formulation of the Lord's Prayer. Similarly, we need not be forced to opt either for Jesus's substitutionary death, in which he deals with sins, or for a representative or liberative death, in which he deals with the power of evil. What therefore God hath joined together, let not man put asunder!

Bibliography

Aulén, G. *Christus Victor: An Historical Study of the Three Main Types of the Idea of the Atonement*. London: SPCK, 1931.

Bailey, D. P. "Concepts of Stellvertretung in the Interpretation of Isaiah 53." In Bellinger and Farmer, *Jesus and the Suffering Servant*, 223–50.

Bammel, C. P. Hammond. "Patristic Exegesis of Romans 5:7." *JTS* 47 (1996): 532–42.

Barth, K. *Church Dogmatics*. Edinburgh: T&T Clark, 1956–75.

Bell, R. H. *Deliver Us from Evil: Interpreting the Redemption from the Power of Satan in New Testament Theology*. Tübingen: Mohr Siebeck, 2007.

———. "Sacrifice and Christology in Paul." *JTS* 53 (2002): 1–27.

Bellinger, W. H., and W. R. Farmer, eds. *Jesus and the Suffering Servant: Isaiah 53 and Christian Origins*. Harrisburg, PA: Trinity, 1998.

Bieringer, R. "Traditionsgeschichtlicher Ursprung und theologische Bedeutung der ὑπέρ-Aussagen im Neuen Testament." In *The Four Gospels 1992: Festschrift Franz Neirynck*. Vol. 1, edited by F. van Segbroeck, C. M. Tuckett, G. van Belle, and J. Verheyden, 219–48. Leuven: Leuven University Press/Peeters, 1992.

Breytenbach, C. "'Christus starb für uns': Zur Tradition und paulinischen Rezeption der sogenannten 'Sterbeformeln.'" *NTS* 49 (2003): 447–75.

———. "The 'For Us' Phrases in Pauline Soteriology: Considering Their Background and Use." In *Salvation in the New Testament: Perspectives on Soteriology*, edited by J. van der Watt, 163–85. Leiden: Brill, 2005.

———. "Jes^{LXX} 53,6.12 als Interpretatio Graeca und die urchristlichen Hingabeformeln." In *Die Septuaginta: Texte, Theologien, Einflüsse*, edited by W. Kraus and M. Karrer, 655–70. WUNT 252. Tübingen: Mohr Siebeck, 2010.

———. "The Septuagint Version of Isaiah 53 and the Early Christian Formula 'He Was Delivered for Our Trespasses.'" *NovT* 51 (2009): 339–51.

———. "Versöhnung, Stellvertretung und Sühne: Semantische und traditionsgeschichtliche Bemerkungen am Beispiel der paulinischen Briefe." *NTS* 39 (1993): 59–79.

Brondos, D. *Paul on the Cross: Reconstructing the Apostle's Story of Redemption*. Minneapolis: Fortress, 2006.

Bultmann, R. *Theologie des Neuen Testaments*. Tübingen: Mohr, 1953.

Calder, W. M., III. "The Alkestis Inscription from Odessos: IGBR I² 222." *AJA* 79 (1975): 80–83.

Campbell, D. A. *The Deliverance of God*. Grand Rapids: Eerdmans, 2009.

———. *The Quest for Paul's Gospel: A Suggested Strategy*. New York: Continuum, 2005.

Chalke, S., and A. Mann. *The Lost Message of Jesus*. Grand Rapids: Zondervan, 2006.

Chaniotis, A. "Illness and Cures in the Greek Propitiatory Inscriptions and Dedications of Lydia and Phrygia." In *Ancient Medicine in Its Socio-Cultural Context: Papers Read at the Congress Held at Leiden University 13–15 April 1992*, edited by H. F. J. Horstmanshoff, P. J. van der Eijk, and P. H. Schrijvers, 2:323–44. Amsterdam: Rodopi, 1995.

Clarke, A. D. "The Good and the Just in Romans 5:7." *TynBul* 41 (1990): 128–42.

Clines, D. J. A. *I, He, We, and They: A Literary Approach to Isaiah 53*. Sheffield: Sheffield Academic Press, 1976.

Crisp, O. "Non-Penal Substitution." *IJST* 9 (2007): 415–33.

Davie, M. "Dead to Sin and Alive to God." *SBET* 19 (2001): 158–94.

de Boer, M. C. *Galatians: A Commentary*. Louisville: Westminster John Knox, 2011.

de Jonge, H. J. "The Original Setting of the Χριστὸς ἀπέθανεν ὑπέρ Formula." In *The Thessalonian Correspondence*, edited by R. F. Collins, 229–35. Leuven: Leuven University Press/Peeters, 1990.

Dunn, J. D. G. "Paul's Understanding of the Death of Jesus as Sacrifice." In *Sacrifice and Redemption: Durham Essays in Theology*, edited by S. W. Sykes, 35–56. Cambridge: Cambridge University Press, 1991.

———. *The Theology of Paul's Letter to the Galatians*. Cambridge: Cambridge University Press, 1993.

———. *The Theology of Paul the Apostle*. Grand Rapids: Eerdmans, 1998.

Dyson, M. "Alcestis' Children and the Character of Admetus." *JHS* 108 (1988): 13–23.

Eastman, S. G. "Apocalypse and Incarnation: The Participatory Logic of Paul's Gospel." In *Apocalyptic and the Future of Theology: With and Beyond J. Louis Martyn*, edited by J. B. Davis and D. Harink, 165–82. Eugene, OR: Wipf & Stock, 2012.

Eriksson, A. *Traditions as Rhetorical Proof: Pauline Argumentation in I Corinthians*. Stockholm: Almquist & Wiksell, 1998.

Eschner, C. "Die Hingabe des einzigen Sohnes ‚für' uns alle. Zur Wiederaufnahme des Sterben-‚für'-Motivs aus Röm 5,6–8 in Röm 8,32." In *The Letter to the Romans*, edited by U. Schnelle, 659–78. Leuven: Leuven University Press/Peeters, 2009.

———. *Gestorben und hingegeben „für" die Sünder: Die griechische Konzeption des Unheil abwendenden Sterbens und deren paulinische Aufnahme für die Deutung des Todes Jesu Christi*. Neukirchen-Vluyn: Neukirchener Verlag, 2010.

Finlan, S. *The Background and Content of Paul's Cultic Atonement Metaphors*. Atlanta: Society of Biblical Literature, 2004.

Fraser, G. "Cross Purposes." *Guardian*, April 4, 2007. http://www.theguardian .com/commentisfree/2007/apr/04/christrecrucified.

Gallo, I. "Vita di Filonide Epicureo." In *Studi di papirologia ercolanese*, 59–205. Naples: M. D'Autia Editore, 2002.

Gathercole, S. J. "Justification by Faith." In *The Oxford Handbook to Paul*, edited by R. B. Matlock. Oxford: Oxford University Press, forthcoming.

———. "Justified by Faith, Justified by His Blood: The Evidence of Romans 3:21–4:25." In *Justification and Variegated Nomism*. Vol. 2, *The Paradoxes of Paul*, edited by D. A. Carson, P. T. O'Brien, and M. A. Seifrid, 147–84. Tübingen: Mohr Siebeck; Grand Rapids: Baker Academic, 2004.

Gaventa, B., ed. *Apocalyptic Paul: Cosmos and Anthropos in Romans 5–8*. Waco: Baylor University Press, 2013.

———. "The Cosmic Power of Sin in Paul's Letter to the Romans: Toward a Widescreen Edition." *Interpretation* 58 (2004): 229–40.

Gese, H. "The Atonement." In *Essays on Biblical Theology*, 93–116. Minneapolis: Augsburg, 1981.

Goldhill, S. D. *Reading Greek Tragedy*. Cambridge: Cambridge University Press, 1986.

Hengel, M. *The Atonement: A Study of the Origins of the Doctrine in the New Testament*. London: SCM, 1981.

Hengel, M., and A. M. Schwemer. *Paul between Damascus and Antioch*. London: SCM, 1997.

Hengel, M., with the collaboration of D. P. Bailey. "The Effective History of Isaiah 53 in the Pre-Christian Period." In Janowski and Stuhlmacher, *Suffering Servant*, 75–146.

Hitchens, C. *God Is Not Great: How Religion Poisons Everything*. London: Atlantic, 2008.

Hitchens, C., and D. Wilson. *Is Christianity Good for the World? A Debate*. Moscow, ID: Canon, 2008.

Hofius, O. "Erwägungen zur Gestalt und Herkunft des paulinischen Versöhnungsgedankens." *ZTK* 77 (1980): 186–99. Reprinted in Hofius, *Paulusstudien*, 1–14.

———. "The Fourth Servant Song in the New Testament Letters." In Janowski and Stuhlmacher, *Suffering Servant*, 163–88.

———. "'Gott hat unter uns aufgerichtet das Wort von der Versöhnung' (2 Kor 5,19)." *ZNW* 71 (1980): 3–20. Reprinted in Hofius, *Paulusstudien*, 15–32.

———. *Paulusstudien*. WUNT 51. Tübingen: Mohr, 1989.

———. "Sühne und Versöhnung: Zum paulinischen Verständnis des Kreuzestodes Jesu." In Hofius, *Paulusstudien*, 33–49.

Holmes, S. "Can Punishment Bring Peace? Penal Substitution Revisited." *SJT* 58 (2005): 104–23.

Hooker, M. D. "Did the Use of Isaiah 53 to Interpret His Mission Begin with Jesus?" In Bellinger and Farmer, *Jesus and the Suffering Servant*, 88–103.

———. *From Adam to Christ: Essays on Paul*. Cambridge: Cambridge University Press, 1990.

———. "Interchange and Atonement." In *From Adam to Christ*, 26–41.

———. "Interchange in Christ." In *From Adam to Christ*, 13–25. Originally published in *JTS* 22 (1971): 349–61.

———. *Jesus and the Servant: The Influence of the Servant Concept of Deutero-Isaiah in the New Testament*. London: SPCK, 1959.

———. *Not Ashamed of the Gospel: New Testament Interpretations of the Death of Christ*. Carlisle: Paternoster, 1994.

———. "On Becoming the Righteousness of God: Another Look at 2 Corinthians 5:21." *NovT* 50 (2008): 358–75.

———. "Paul the Pastor: The Relevance of the Gospel." PIBA 31 (2009): 17–31.

———. *A Preface to Paul*. New York: Oxford University Press, 1980.

Janowski, B. "He Bore Our Sins: Isaiah 53 and the Drama of Taking Another's Place." In Janowski and Stuhlmacher, *Suffering Servant*, 48–74.

Janowski, B., and P. Stuhlmacher, eds. *The Suffering Servant: Isaiah 53 in Jewish and Christian Sources*. Grand Rapids: Eerdmans, 2004.

Jeffery, S., M. Ovey, and A. Sach, eds. *Pierced for Our Transgressions: Rediscovering the Glory of Penal Substitution*. Leicester: Apollos, 2007.

Jewett, R. *Romans: A Commentary*. Hermeneia. Minneapolis: Fortress, 2006.

Kant, I. *Religion within the Boundaries of Mere Reason*. In *Religion and Rational Theology*, edited by A. Wood and G. Di Giovanni, 57–215. Cambridge Edition of the Works of Immanuel Kant. Cambridge: Cambridge University Press, 1996.

Käsemann, E. *New Testament Questions of Today*. London: SCM, 1979.

———. "Zum Verständnis von Römer 3,24–26." *ZNW* 43 (1950–51): 150–54.

Kertelge, K. "Das Verständnis des Todes Jesu bei Paulus." In *Der Tod Jesu: Deutungen im Neuen Testament*, edited by J. Beutler, 114–36. Freiburg: Herder, 1976.

Kloppenborg, J. S. "An Analysis of the Pre-Pauline Formula 1 Cor 15:3b–5 in Light of Some Recent Literature." *CBQ* 40 (1978): 351–67.

Koester, H. "The Structure and Criteria of Early Christian Beliefs." In *Trajectories through Early Christianity*, edited by J. M. Robinson and H. Koester, 205–31. Philadelphia: Fortress, 1971.

Landau, Y. "Martyrdom in Paul's Religious Ethics: An Exegetical Commentary on Romans 5:7." *Immanuel: Ecumenical Theological Research Fraternity (Jerusalem)* 15 (1982–83): 24–38.

Lennox, J. *Gunning for God: Why the New Atheists Are Missing the Target*. Oxford: Lion, 2011.

Letham, R. *The Work of Christ*. Leicester: Inter-Varsity, 1993.

Lewis, C. S. *The Four Loves*. London: Geoffrey Bles, 1960.

Lohse, E. *Märtyrer und Gottesknecht: Untersuchungen zur urchristlichen Verkündigung vom Sühntod Jesu Christi*. Göttingen: Vandenhoeck & Ruprecht, 1963.

Martin, R. P. "Center of Paul's Theology." In *Dictionary of Paul and His Letters*, edited by G. Hawthorne, R. P. Martin, and D. Reid, 92–95. Leicester: Inter-Varsity, 1993.

Martin, T. W. "The Good as God (Rom. 5:7)." *JSNT* 25 (2002): 55–70.

Martyn, J. L. *Galatians*. Anchor Bible 33A. New Haven: Yale University Press, 1997.

———. *Theological Issues in the Letters of Paul*. Edinburgh: T&T Clark, 1997.

Matlock, R. B. "Zeal for Paul but Not according to Knowledge: Douglas Campbell's War on 'Justification Theory.'" *JSNT* 34 (2011): 115–49.

Moule, C. F. D. *An Idiom Book of New Testament Greek*. Cambridge: Cambridge University Press, 1959.

Murray, A.T., trans. *Homer: Iliad, Books 1–12*. Revised by W. F. Wyatt. LCL. Cambridge, MA: Harvard University Press, 1999.

Oldfather, C. H. *Diodorus Siculus: Library of History, Volume IV, Books 9–12.40*. LCL. Cambridge, MA: Harvard University Press, 1946.

Ovey, M. "The Cross, Creation and the Human Predicament." In *Where Wrath and Mercy Meet: Preaching the Atonement Today*, edited by D. Peterson, 100–135. Carlisle: Paternoster, 2002.

Pelikan, J., ed. *Luther's Works*. Vol. 26, *Lectures on Galatians (1535)*. St. Louis: Concordia, 1968.

Plevnik, J. "The Center of Paul's Theology." *CBQ* 51 (1989): 460–78.

Powers, D. G. *Salvation through Participation: An Examination of the Notion of the Believers' Corporate Unity with Christ in Early Christian Soteriology*. Leuven: Peeters, 2001.

Quinn, P. L. "Christian Atonement and Kantian Justification." *Faith and Philosophy* 3 (1986): 440–62.

Rist, J. M. "Epicurus on Friendship." *Classical Philology* 75 (1980): 121–29.

Röhser, G. *Stellvertretung im Neuen Testament*. Stuttgart: Verlag Katholisches Bibelwerk, 2002.

Rossi, P. "Kant's Philosophy of Religion." *Stanford Encyclopedia of Philosophy*. http://plato.stanford.edu/entries/kant-religion/.

Sanders, E. P. *Paul and Palestinian Judaism*. Minneapolis: Fortress, 1977.

Schreiner, T. R. *Apostle of God's Glory in Christ*. Leicester: Inter-Varsity, 2001.

Seeberg, A. *Der Katechismus der Urchristenheit*. Leipzig: Deichert, 1903.

Shaw, D. A. B. "Apocalyptic and Covenant: Perspectives on Paul or Antinomies at War?" *JSNT* 36 (2013): 155–71.

Snyder Belousek, D. W. *Atonement, Justice, and Peace: The Message of the Cross and the Mission of the Church*. Grand Rapids: Eerdmans, 2012.

Sourvinou-Inwood, C. "Iphigenia." OCD^3, 765–66.

Stanton, G. N. *The Gospels and Jesus*. 2nd ed. Oxford: Oxford University Press, 2002.

Stendahl, K. *Paul among Jews and Gentiles*. Minneapolis: Fortress, 1976.

Stott, J. R. W. *The Cross of Christ*. Leicester: Inter-Varsity, 2006.

Strecker, G. *Theology of the New Testament*. Louisville: Westminster John Knox, 2000.

Thiselton, A. C. *The First Epistle to the Corinthians*. NIGTC. Carlisle: Paternoster, 2000.

Versnel, H. S. "Making Sense of Jesus' Death: The Pagan Contribution." In *Deutungen des Todes Jesu im Neuen Testament*, edited by J. Frey and J. Schröter, 215–94. WUNT 181. Tübingen: Mohr Siebeck, 2005.

————. "Self-Sacrifice, Compensation and the Anonymous Gods." In *Le sacrifice dans l'antiquité*, by J.-P. Vernant et al., 135–94. Geneva: Vandœvres, 1980.

Weaver, J. D. *The Non-Violent Atonement*. Grand Rapids: Eerdmans, 2011.

Weiss, J. *Das Urchristentum*. Göttingen: Vandenhoeck & Ruprecht, 1917.

————. *Der erste Korintherbrief*. KEK. Göttingen: Vandenhoeck & Ruprecht, 1909.

Wengst, K. *Christologische Formeln und Lieder des Urchristentums*. Gütersloh: Gütersloher Verlagshaus, 1972.

Wenz, G. *Geschichte der Versöhnungslehre in der evangelischen Theologie der Neuzeit*. Münchener Monographien zur historischen und systematischen Theologie. Munich: Kaiser, 1984.

Williams, S. K. *Jesus' Death as Saving Event: The Background and Origin of a Concept*. Missoula, MT: Scholars Press, 1975.

Wisse, F. "The Righteous Man and the Good Man in Romans V.7." *NTS* 19 (1972–73): 91–93.

Wolter, M. "Der Heilstod Jesu als theologisches Argument." In *Deutungen des Todes Jesu im Neuen Testament*, edited by J. Frey and J. Schröter, 297–314. Tübingen: Mohr Siebeck, 2005.

Wood, S. "Alcestis on Roman Sarcophagi." *AJA* 82 (1978): 499–510.

Wright, N. T. *Paul and the Faithfulness of God*. London: SPCK, 2013.

Zahl, S. "Atonement." In *The Oxford Handbook of Theology and Modern European Thought*, edited by N. Adams, G. Pattison, and G. Ward, 633–54. Oxford: Oxford University Press, 2013.

Ziesler, J. A. *Paul's Letter to the Romans*. London: SCM, 1989.

Index of Subjects

"apocalyptic" interpretation, 42–47, 53–54, 110

Christology, 24–25
Christus Victor. *See* "apocalyptic" interpretation
classical parallels, 90–107

Day of Atonement, 30–38
death, 27–28, 32, 80–83
  of Christians, 80–83
  as "perishing," 81–83
  as "sleep," 81, 82
debt, 26–27. *See also* payment
"dying" formulae, 55–56

Epicureans, 101–2, 105

friendship, 97–101

God
  freedom of, 27
  love of, 103–5, 111
  mercy of, 27
  and Trinity, 24–25
gospel, 14, 50, 53, 57–59, 77–78, 111
guilt, 16, 17, 19, 26–27, 35–36, 38, 40, 46, 47, 54, 62, 63, 69, 76

Hebrew Bible. *See* Scripture
heroism, 87, 92–94, 95, 97, 104, 106

identification, 31–32
inclusive substitution, 33–35, 75–77. *See also* "Tübingen" interpretation
interchange, 38–42, 53–54, 110
Iphigenia, 21
Israel, 19, 22, 31, 33, 37, 43, 51, 60, 62, 63, 70, 111

Kantianism, 22, 24, 26–27, 35, 38, 120, 122

Law, the, 15, 16, 43, 44, 45, 79, 88. *See also* Scripture
Lord's Prayer, 113
love
  of Christ, 103–5
  conjugal, 91–97
  and friendship, 97–101

objections to substitution
  and Christians' deaths, 27–28, 80–83
  immorality, 24–25
  legal fiction, 23–24
  philosophical-ethical, 26–27. *See also* Kantianism
Old Testament. *See* Scripture

patriotic death, 89–91
Paul
    center of theology of, 78
    and gospel. *See* gospel
    and pre-Pauline tradition, 43–44, 47–48,
        51–53
payment, 22. *See also* debt
penalty, 18–20
prepositions, 73–74, 79
prohibitions of substitution, 70–72
propitiation, 21–22
Pythagoreans, 97–98, 102

representation, 13–14, 20, 23, 29, 109,
    111–13
resurrection, 60–61

sacrifice. *See* Day of Atonement
satisfaction, 22
scapegoat, 22, 37
Scripture, 56–72, 86
sins, 17, 38, 42, 44, 47–53, 55–79
Stoics, 100, 102, 104–5
substitution
    definition of, 15–18
    importance of, 14–15
Suffering Servant, 61–70, 86

"Tübingen" interpretation, 30–38, 53–54,
    75–77, 109–10

Index of Authors

Adams, N., 25
Aulén, G., 52

Bailey, D. P., 19, 26, 30, 33, 62, 66
Barth, K., 15, 17
Bell, R. H., 30, 33, 35
Belle, G. van, 56
Bellinger, W. H., 33, 63
Beutler, J., 77
Bieringer, R., 56, 67, 74
Boer, M. C. de, 44–45
Breytenbach, C., 38, 56, 74–75, 87, 88, 97
Brondos, D., 80
Bultmann, R., 52

Calder, W. M., 96, 97
Calvin, J., 14
Campbell, D. A., 23, 45–46, 59, 112
Carnley, P., 24, 26
Carson, D. A., 18
Cavallo, G., 102
Chalke, S., 24, 26
Chaniotis, A., 21
Clarke, A. D., 87–89
Clines, D. J. A., 68
Crim, K., 33
Crisp, O., 19

Davie, M., 14
Davis, J. B., 44
Dawkins, R., 25
Di Giovanni, G., 26
Dunn, J. D. G., 37, 48, 54
Dyson, M., 92–94

Eastman, S. G., 44, 45
Eijk, P. J. van der, 22
Eriksson, A., 60, 67
Eschner, C., 55, 60, 66, 67, 86, 88

Farmer, W. R., 33, 63
Finlan, S., 18
Fraser, G., 22
Frey, J., 67, 91, 100

Gallo, I., 102
Gaventa, B., 42, 44
Gese, H., 30–38, 75
Goldhill, S. D., 98, 99

Hammond Bammel, C. P., 87–89
Harink, D., 44
Hengel, M., 58, 66, 67
Hitchens, C., 27
Hofius, O., 30, 33–36, 47, 48, 70, 75–77
Holmes, S., 24, 28

Hooker, M. D., 38–42, 47, 59, 63, 80
Horstmanshoff, H. F. J., 22

Janowski, B., 26, 27, 30, 61–63, 66, 70
Jeffery, S., 37
Jewett, R., 29

Kant, I., 26–27, 35, 38
Karrer, M., 66
Käsemann, E., 52, 78
Kertelge, K., 77
Kloppenborg, J. S., 68
Koester, H., 67–68
Kraus, W., 66

Landau, Y., 87, 95
Lennox, J., 25
Letham, R., 15, 17
Lewis, C. S., 103
Lohse, E., 52
Luther, M., 15–17

Mann, A., 24
Martin, T. W., 87–88
Martyn, J. L., 42–47, 51, 52
Matlock, R. B., 112
McLeod Campbell, J., 19
Moule, C. F. D., 89

O'Brien, P. T., 18
Oldfather, C. H., 98
Orlinsky, H. M., 68
Ovey, M., 24, 37

Pattison, G., 25
Pelikan, J., 16
Peterson, D., 24
Plevnik, J., 78
Powers, D. G., 29

Quinn, P. L., 26, 27

Reid, D., 78
Rist, J. M., 101
Robinson, J. M., 68
Röhser, G., 14, 18, 25, 26, 27, 37
Rossi, P., 26

Sach, A., 37
Schlatter, A., 34
Schnelle, U., 66
Schreiner, T. R., 78
Schrijvers, P. H., 22
Schröter, J., 67, 91, 100
Schwemer, A.-M., 58
Seeberg, A., 51
Segbroeck, F. van, 56
Seifrid, M. A., 18
Shakespeare, W., 19
Shaw, D. A. B., 46
Snaith, N. H., 68
Snyder Belousek, D. W., 18
Sourvinou-Inwood, C., 21
Stanton, G. N., 52
Stendahl, K., 50–51
Stott, J. R. W., 24
Strecker, G., 52
Stuhlmacher, P., 26, 30, 62, 66, 70
Sykes, S. W., 54

Thiselton, A. C., 58
Tuckett, C. M., 56

Verheyden, J., 56
Vernant, J.-P., 95
Versnel, H. S., 67, 72, 91, 95–96, 97

Ward, G., 25
Warren, J., 101
Watt, J. van der, 39, 56, 87
Weiss, J., 51
Wenz, G., 26
Williams, S. K., 66, 68
Wilson, D., 27
Wisse, F., 87
Wolter, M., 100
Wood, A., 26
Wood, S., 97
Wright, N. T., 111
Wyatt, W. F., 99

Zahl, S., 25
Ziesler, J. A., 53

Index of Scripture
and Other Ancient Sources

Old Testament

Exodus

23:7 24

Leviticus

4 37
4–5 31
4:4 20
5:11–13 31
16 31–34, 37
16:5 38
16:21–22 37
26:34–35 22

Numbers

27 70
27:3 70

Deuteronomy

24:16 71

Joshua

22:20 70–71

1 Samuel

2:6–7 60

1 Kings

16:18–19 (LXX)
    70, 71, 74

2 Chronicles

25:4 71
29 37
29:5 37
29:21 37
29:23 37
29:31 37

Psalms

32:1 50, 51

Isaiah

40 62, 111
40:2 22
42 62
42:18–19 62
42:20 62
44:21 62
46 62
52:4 64
52:5 64
52:7 64
52:13 65
52:15 64
53 61–72, 110
53:1 64, 68
53:3 69
53:4 65
53:4–5 69
53:5 65, 69
53:6 64, 65
53:7 65, 69
53:8 65, 66, 67, 69
53:9 69
53:11 65
53:12 16, 64, 65,
    66, 67, 69
59:20 50

Jeremiah

31:30 71
38:30 LXX 71

Ezekiel

3:18 70
3:18–20 70
18:17–18 70
18:24 70
18:26 70
33:8–9 70
33:13 70
33:18 70

Hosea

6:2 60–61

New Testament

Matthew

6:12–13 113
9:24 81
12:40 60
26:28 67

Mark

5:39 81
10:45 52
14:24 67

Luke

8:52 81

John

11:11–13 81
18:8–9 13

Acts

2:36 72
3:18–20 111

Romans

1–3 46
1–4 46
1:3–4 52
1:16–17 57
1:18 49
1:22–23 105
1:30 49
1:32 82
2:9 49
2:12 50
2:23 49
2:24 64
3:7 50
3:8 49
3:23 50
3:25 42, 49, 50, 52
3:25–26 52
4:6–8 50
4:7 49, 50

4:8 49, 50
4:15 49
4:25 51, 52, 63–64,
      65, 67, 75,
      76, 82
5–8 46
5:6 86–107
5:6–8 55, 85–107,
      111
5:6–9 42
5:7 86–107
5:7–8 87
5:8 50, 86–107
5:9 47
5:9–10 106
5:10 104
5:12–21 50
5:14 49, 50
5:15 49
5:16 49, 50
5:17 49
5:18 49
5:19 49, 50
6 14, 81
6:5 83
6:8 13, 60
6:15 50
6:21 82
6:23 82
7:5 49
7:19 49
8:3 42
8:6 81
8:13 49, 81, 82
8:32 64
9:11 49
10:15 64
10:16 64
11:26 49, 50
11:27 49, 50
11:30 49
12:17 49
13:3 49
13:4 49
13:10 49
13:12 49
14:8 81
14:23 49
15:21 64

1 Corinthians

1–2 41
1:18 82
1:23 42
2:2 42
6:8 50
6:18 49
7:28 50
7:39 81
8:11 67
8:12 50
10:6 49
11:23–26 51
11:30 81
13:5 49
15:1 57
15:1–4 111
15:1–11 57–59
15:2 58
15:3 49, 50, 53,
      55–79, 83, 85,
      86, 110, 111,
      112
15:3–4 57, 58, 59,
      75, 78
15:3–5 51, 57, 78
15:4 60
15:6 81
15:11 58
15:17 48, 49
15:18 81
15:20 81
15:22 81
15:26 112
15:34 50
15:36 81
15:51 81

2 Corinthians

2:15 82
2:16 82
4:3 82
4:11–12 81
5:14–15 38
5:14–21 36
5:18–19 53
5:19 34, 36, 49, 50

5:21 39, 41
6:17 64
7:2 50
7:12 50
8:9 39, 41
10:6 49
11:7 49
12:13 49
13:2 50
13:7 49

Galatians

1:1–5 51
1:4 25, 42, 44–45,
     49, 50, 51–53,
     65, 67, 75, 76,
     77, 82, 111
2:15 50
2:17 50
2:20 25, 82
3:13 16, 42, 45–46
3:19 49
5:19 49
6:1 49

Ephesians

2:1 49
5:14 81

Philippians

1:20–21 81
1:23 81
3:19 82

Colossians

1:14 49
2:13–15 47, 112

1 Thessalonians

1 47
1:10 51
2:16 49
4:13 81
4:13–18 82–83
4:14 81

4:15 81
5:10 60, 67, 81
5:22 49
5:25 49

1 Timothy

1:9 50
1:15 50
5:22 49
5:24 49

2 Timothy

3:6 50

Hebrews

4 14
11:5 83

Early Jewish Literature

1 Maccabees

2:50

4 Maccabees

6:22 90

Philo

De specialibus legibus

3.153–54 71

Prayer of Manasseh

7 72

Patristic Literature

Irenaeus

Against Heresies

5, preface 39

Classical (Greek and Latin) Literature

Cicero

De officiis

3.45 97

Tusculanae disputationes

5.22 97

Diodorus Siculus

Bibliotheca historica

10.4 98

Diogenes Laertius

Vitae philosophorum

7.130 100
10.121 101

Epictetus

Dissertationes

2.7.3 100

Epicurus

Frag. 590 [Usener] 101

Euripides

Alcestis

10 94
11–14 92
18 92
284 92
304–5 93
328–30 94
334–35 94

336–37 92
348–56 92
363–68 93
377–78 94
682 92
690 92
701–2 92
855–60 92, 93
950–54 94
1056–61 94

Greek Anthology

7.691 96

Homer

Iliad

6.215–31 99

Hyginus

Fabulae

257 97

Iamblichus

Life of Pythagoras

233–36 97

Life of Philonides

P. Hercul. 1044, frag. 22, lines 7–11 102

Lucian

Toxaris

36 100

Lysias

Against Eratosthenes

78.4–5 71

Musonius Rufus

Discourses

14 96

Plato

Symposium

179b–c 95

Plutarch

Moralia

761E 95

Seneca

Epistles

9.10 100

Inscriptions

IG

XIV 607 95

IGBulg I²

222, lines 11–14 96

Papyri

Papyrus Herculanensis

1044 102